Ethics and Markets

Co-operation and Competition within Capitalist Economies

Ethics and Markets

Co-operation and Competition within Capitalist Economies

Edited by

Colin Crouch and David Marquand

Blackwell Publishers

Copyright © The Political Quarterly Publishing Co. Ltd.

ISBN 0–631–19033–3

First published 1993

Blackwell Publishers
108 Cowley Road, Oxford, OX4 1JF, UK.

and
238 Main Street,
Cambridge, MA. 02142, USA.

British Library Cataloguing in Publication Data
Applied for
ISBN 0–631–19033–3

Library of Congress Cataloguing in Publication Data
Ethics and markets: co-operation and competition within capitalist economies/edited by Colin Crouch and David Marquand.
p.   cm.
Includes index.
ISBN 0–631–19033–3 (pbk.)
1. International economic relations—Moral and ethical aspects.
2. International cooperation.   3. Competition, International.
4. Capitalism—Moral and ethical aspects.   I. Crouch, Colin.
II. Marquand, David.
HF1359.E84   1993   337—dc20   93–19171   CIP

Typeset by Joshua Associates Ltd., Oxford
Printed in Great Britain by Whitstable Litho, Kent.

CONTENTS

Introduction   1
COLIN CROUCH and DAVID MARQUAND

The Moral Boundaries of the Market   6
RUSSELL KEAT

The New Politics of Economics   21
DAVID MILIBAND

Reticulated Organisations: The Birth and Death of the
Mixed Economy   31
GEOFF MULGAN

Catholicism, Christian Democrats and 'Reformed Capitalism'   48
JONATHAN BOSWELL

What Makes the Japanese Different?   66
RONALD DORE

Co-operation and Competition in an Institutionalized
Economy: the Case of Germany   80
COLIN CROUCH

Human Resources and Human Ingenuity   99
JUDITH MARQUAND

Trade Unions and New Managerial Techniques   111
DAVID NORMAN

The Informal Politics of the European Community   126
KEITH MIDDLEMAS

Whither Global Capitalism?   138
WILL HUTTON

Index   147

INTRODUCTION

A SPECTRE is haunting the English-speaking world, the spectre of what Michel Albert has called 'Rhenish' capitalism.[1] As is the wont of spectres, it is a little fuzzy at the edges. As Albert uses it, the term has little to do with geography; 'Rhenish' capitalism is the kind of capitalism—competitive, but at the same time collaborative; market-based but not wholly market-driven—that flourishes in the Germanic lands of central Europe, in Scandinavia and also in Japan. According to Albert, it differs in crucially important ways from the kind of capitalism found in Britain and the United States, a kind which he calls 'neo-American'.

On that level, these two varieties of capitalism have much in common. After all, both are capitalist. In both, the means of production are largely in private hands; in both, resources are allocated largely through the market; both are dominated by private, profit-seeking firms which compete for custom and stand or fall by their ability to pass the tests of the market-place. In a struggle between capitalism and socialism, both are therefore on the same side.

But, says Albert, it is only because that struggle has loomed so large for so long that we have failed to see that, in most other respects, the 'neo-American' and 'Rhenish' models are not merely different, but antagon-istic. For the subtleties of 'Rhenish' capitalism elude the familiar categories of the mainstream Anglo-American economic tradition. They cannot be captured by Ricardians or neo-Ricardians; nor, for that matter, can they be captured by Keynesians or neo-Keynesians. 'Rhenish' capitalism is, of course, competitive. The yardstick of profitability has to be satisfied. But it depends on a subtle symbiosis of competition and co-operation, under-pinned by corporatist or quasi-corporatist institutions and practices which the neo-classical economic doctrines of the Anglo-American tradition would condemn as protectionist and therefore inefficient. In short, its market is not the famous 'undistorted' market of the Anglo-American economics profession and the Anglo-American political class. What the Anglo-American tradition sees as distortions, impeding free competition, it sees as the necessary conditions of competitive success.

And—in some respects the crucial point—success has been spectacu-larly forthcoming. For the obvious competitive power of the capitalisms of Germany and Japan is not fortuitous. It is directly related to the features of the German and Japanese political economies which the Anglo-American economic tradition cannot encompass, and which commentators brought up in that tradition find alien, or shocking, or both. For the point about 'Rhenish' capitalism is that the market does not operate in the way that

---

[1] Michel Albert, *Capitalisme Contre Capitalisme*, Editions du Seuil, Paris, 1991.

Anglo-American tradition presupposes; that it is not driven by individual self-interest and the search for profit in the short term; that market forces are constrained by dense and complex networks of intersecting interests, held together by solidaristic values and co-operative habits.

Because of all this, market actors are able to take a long view—above all, in respect of human capital. The system as a whole trades off losses in the short-term efficiency on which the Anglo-American tradition focuses against gains in consensual adaptation and social peace. It owes its extraordinary success to its capacity to make that trade-off. For, in a sophisticated economy, human capital holds the key to competitive power; and the more important human capital becomes, the less appropriate is a model of economic behaviour drawn from the Anglo-American tradition. The mill owners of early-nineteenth-century Lancashire could and did treat their under-educated, unskilled 'hands' as factors of production and nothing more, as subject to the laws of political economy as a bale of cotton. If the skilled technicians of an advanced modern economy are treated in the same way, if their relations with capital are regulated exclusively by the calculus of the market, they will soon discover that it pays them to use their market power, while they have it, to extract a monopoly rent from the rest of us and to slow adaptation down. In a high-skilled—or would-be high-skilled—economy, consensual adaptation and social peace are public goods, for which it is worth paying a price in strict allocative efficiency. By the same token, the possessive, inevitably short-term, individualism that drives the Anglo-American model becomes self-stultifying.

A British Clintonomics?

In the era of triumphalist 'Reaganomics' and 'Thatcheromics' such arguments cut little ice in the English-speaking world. But that era is now over. Whatever may have been true of the halcyon mid-1980s, it is beyond dispute that the capitalisms of Britain and the United States have been exceptionally vulnerable to the storms of the 1990s. President Clinton owed his election, at least in part, to a critique of American capitalism, developed by advisers like Robert Reich, which had much in common with Michel Albert's. Partly because the Labour Party cannot easily abandon its ancestral suspicion of any form of capitalism—whether 'Rhenish' or otherwise—and partly because the Liberal Democrats have tried so hard to love the market that they are afraid of looking ridiculous if they start to question it, the British debate is still a long way behind the American. No British political leader has yet offered a coherent British version of 'Clintonomics', and it would be rash to assume that any British political leader will do so in the short or medium term.

What this shows, however, is that there is a vacuum waiting to be filled. The failure of British capitalism is palpable—more palpable, if anything,

2

than the failure of its American *alter ego*. No one outside the diminished ranks of Labour's Old Left believe that salvation lies in anything that could remotely be described as socialism. The core socialist assumption that social ownership was bound to be more efficient than private, and social direction than the market, has turned out to be the reverse of the truth. Apart from the Cubans everyone now accepts that it is social ownership, not private, which fetters the productive powers of modern industry; that direction, not the market, produces the most grotesque misallocations and the most crippling bottlenecks. The ethic of socialism is as compelling as ever, but its economics are hopelessly discredited. If there is any solution at all to Britain's economic problems (and no divine law decrees that there must be), it can only lie in a different form of capitalism.

Hence this book. It is intended to contribute to, and if possible to help to stimulate, a debate about the lessons to be learned from the successful capitalisms of Germany and Japan; about the ways in which changes in the international environment are likely to constrain the choices open to any would-be British 'Clintonomist'; and, on a deeper level, about the moral and ideological foundations on which a project designed to turn British capitalism around would have to build.

The last point deserves particular attention. In Britain (though not in the United States), books about political economy rarely address ideological or ethical questions. Partly because the academic division of labour has tended to insulate specialists in a subject known as 'political theory' from other social scientists, and partly because a certain coarse-grained behaviourism pervades the academic as well as the political culture, the relationship between economic behaviour on the one hand, and political ideology and moral values on the other, has been under-explored. This neglect, it is worth noting, would have surprised the founding fathers of classical political economy no less than the founding fathers of sociology and political science. Smith and Marshall knew as well as Marx and Weber that economic behaviour and political and ethical beliefs are closely connected. But in our time, at least in the United Kingdom, the elementary truth that economic agents are also bearers of moral and political values, and shaped by moral and political traditions, is often forgotten.

As Ronald Dore points out in his chapter, at least two of the factors which have helped to generate and sustain the Japanese form of capitalism have to do with ideas and beliefs. One is the presence of a 'productivist' ethic, which holds that 'producing goods and services which enhance the lives of others is good', while 'spending one's life in the speculative purchase and sales of financial claims is bad'. The other is the absence of the neo-classical economic tradition, which, under the guise of dispassionate analysis, insistently propagates the moral desirability of the Anglo-American way of organising society. Much the same is true of Germany, though, of course, in different ways. As Jonathan Boswell argues, social Catholic moral teaching helped to lay the intellectual *and behavioural* foundations of the reformed capitalism of the post-war period; as Colin

3

Crouch shows, the interlocking institutions which underpin the German form of collaborative capitalism embody and transmit solidaristic values inherited from Germany's pre-industrial past. And, as Russell Keat suggests, the question of where to place the boundaries of the market, of which social domains should be governed by market principles and which other principles, is itself a moral one.

The institutional environment

Moralising in an institutional and historical vacuum is not, however, likely to get us very far. It is not difficult to mount a case for collaborative capitalism based on the 'productivist' ethic that Ronald Dore describes, or, more generally, a moral case against the 'imperialism' of the market that Russell Keat anatomises. There is at least some evidence—ranging from the explosion of popular anger that greeted the Major Government's pit closure programme in late 1992 to the survey data assembled in the British Social Attitude Surveys—that the British public is receptive to arguments of this sort. The trouble is that, in a society without the institutional underpinning that sustains collaborative capitalism in the countries of its birth, a moral critique of the existing economic system is apt to seem airy-fairy or pie-in-the-sky, even to those who find it persuasive in principle. Sermons are for Sundays, not weekdays. Arguments that take the form of a call for repentance, unconnected to institutional reality, can sound suspiciously like sermons.

If British capitalism is to be turned around, it is not enough to show that it ought to be. It is also necessary to show that it can be. That is not a reason for despair. As Judith Marquand shows, some of the institutional changes made in the crucially important training field in the 1980s—changes presided over by neo-liberal ministers whose instincts were much closer to the Anglo-American than to the German or Japanese models of capitalism—point in a broadly 'collaborative' direction. On a different level, the complex, Gruyère-cheese-like processes of the European Community which Keith Middlemas describes, and in which Britain is, and will remain, inextricably caught up, are also more congruent with Germanic than with Anglo-American capitalism. Triumphalist high Thatcherism proclaimed its intention to entrench an 'enterprise culture' derived from an over-simplified version of the 'neo-American' model, but it would be unwise to take on trust its claim to have succeeded. Institutional reality may not be as hostile to collaborative capitalism as its enemies hope or its champions fear. What is needed is to build on the elements in our institutional inheritance which are friendly towards it, and to put the case for it in terms of those elements.

* * *

INTRODUCTION

Since its foundation in 1930, *The Political Quarterly* has tried to explore issues of emerging public importance in both Britain and elsewhere, mainly but by no means exclusively from a left-of-centre point of view. It does this primarily through its regular quarterly pages, but also through occasional conferences and seminars or, as in the present case, through a book devoted to a question of particular topicality and importance.

C.C.
D.M.
The Editors,
The Political Quarterly

5

THE MORAL BOUNDARIES OF THE MARKET

RUSSELL KEAT*

Now that the political and theoretical contest between market and state seems largely settled to the former's advantage, at least for the foreseeable future, it is perhaps easier to focus on some important issues about the nature and place of economic markets which have often been obscured by the intensity of that contest.

First, there are questions about the specific character that a market economy might take, including both the broad contrast between capitalist and non-capitalist forms, and finer-grained distinctions between particular versions of each.[1] I shall have little to say about these questions, beyond declaring at the outset my allegiance to the kind of non-capitalist, market socialism recently articulated by writers such as David Miller,[2] whilst also registering my belief that even within the broad category of capitalist market economies, there remains a number of morally significant differences between their particular forms.

Second, there are questions about the precise scope of the market domain: about how, and upon what basis, the boundaries should be drawn around the domain of activities to be governed by the market. These questions arise whatever the specific character of a market economy may be and can thus be tackled in a largely independent manner. It is these that I shall explore in this paper. And I shall do so primarily through a critical commentary on Michael Walzer's illuminating discussion of them in his *Spheres of Justice*.[3] But in order to contextualise the kind of approach that I shall be taking, I begin by briefly identifying some of the main directions taken in other work that has addressed, at least implicitly, the problem of market boundaries.

* Russell Keat is Reader in Social Philosophy at Lancaster University. As Director of the University's interdisciplinary Centre for the Study of Cultural Values, he has been closely involved in its recent research on enterprise culture and contemporary forms of consumerism. He has also served for many years as a member of the editorial board of *Radical Philosophy*.

[1] Some of these variations involve different relations between the private sector and the state, differences that are explored elsewhere in this volume; my opening paragraph concerns only the two primary forms of economic organisation.

[2] David Miller, *Market, State and Community*, Oxford University Press, Oxford, 1989; see also the papers in Julian Le Grand and Saul Estrin, eds., *Market Socialism*, Oxford University Press, Oxford, 1989.

[3] Martin Robertson, London, 1983. There has been little discussion of this aspect of Walzer's book (see especially Chapter 4) in the critical literature, most of which has focused instead on its conception of social critique. An exception is Chapter 3 of Michael Rustin's *For a Pluralist Socialism*, Verso, London, 1985.

Perhaps unsurprisingly, one finds rather little explicit discussion of this problem by the more enthusiastic supporters of market economies. It is as if their theoretical energy has been so fully utilised in demonstrating the virtues of the market that little has been left to deal with the arguably prior question of what it is that defines the nature—and hence limits—of that 'economic' domain with respect to which market and state are seen as the chief and rival contenders. Yet even here one often finds some recognition of a broad separation between economic, political and personal domains: for example, in Friedman's argument that the market is a necessary condition for the existence of a liberal-democratic political system; and in Hayek's arguments against the applicability to the market of conceptions of justice, based on merit or desert, that belong only to personal or family life.[4]

Turning now to less whole-hearted proponents of the market— including advocates of market socialism—one can identify a number of distinct concerns amongst those who have addressed this question of market boundaries.[5] First, there are those who have argued, from the standpoint of (typically needs-based) principles of distributive justice, that goods such as health care and education should be provided on a non-market basis—a claim with which I entirely agree, merely noting that the greater the cultural significance of market-provided goods, the more compelling is the case for such non-market provision.[6]

Secondly, there is the continuing concern with a wide (and seemingly ever-expanding!) range of 'market-failures', including both those involving the under-provision of public goods, and those due to the existence of various kinds of externalities. The latter, especially, have gained increasing attention in recent discussions of environmental decision-making, including the use of cost-benefit analyses as an alternative or supplement to market mechanisms.

Finally, there has been a long-standing debate about the moral propriety or otherwise of the sale and purchase of various items of an especially intimate, and often corporeal nature, including blood, bodily organs, and both reproductive and sexual services—a debate in which Titmuss's study of blood-provision has become a major reference-point,[7] and which has been further fuelled both by more recent developments in

---

[4] See Milton Friedman, *Capitalism and Freedom*, University of Chicago Press, Chicago, 1962; and Friedrich Hayek, *The Constitution of Liberty*, Routledge and Kegan Paul, London, 1960.

[5] One could distinguish here between those who ascribe some positive value to the market and those who do not—who regard it as a 'necessary evil', as it were. For the latter, defining market boundaries is an exercise in damage-limitation; for the former, it is a matter of 'keeping it in its place'.

[6] Including, as Walzer neatly argues, the provision of money itself, the means to engage in the culturally valued activity of consumption: *op. cit.*, pp. 103–108.

[7] Richard Titmuss, *The Gift Relationship*, Allen and Unwin, London, 1970; see also Peter Singer, 'Altruism and Commerce: A Defense of Titmuss against Arrow', *Philosophy and Public Affairs*, vol. 2, 1973, pp. 312–320.

7

bio-technology and by the rise of strongly libertarian defences of the free market.

It is probably this last kind of case that would most commonly be seen as involving distinctively moral issues about market boundaries, together perhaps with those involving questions of distributive justice.[8] But I shall have little to say about either of these. Instead my focus will mainly be on that broad separation between personal, political and economic domains noted above, and more specifically on the need to expand this rather minimal schema to make room for domains other than the personal and political that may also require protection from the market, and hence boundaries to be set around it.

In particular I have in mind the domain(s) consisting in social practices and institutions of a broadly cultural character: broadcasting and journalism, museums and the arts, education, sports, academic research and many others. These include, of course, many of those institutions that in Britain today, despite the apparent demise both of Lord Young and of the political rhetoric of 'enterprise culture', continue to be subject to the extension of market or quasi-market forces and the introduction of commercially modelled forms of organisation.[9]

Further, I suggest, the issues raised by these kinds of changes may also properly be seen as moral or ethical ones, despite the more usual restriction of these terms to the cases noted earlier. The approach I shall be taking reflects the growing tendency in current moral philosophy to revive a broadly Aristotelian conception of the discipline, according to which the central question is 'what is the good life for humans?', and any adequate answer will include the identification of various, often institutionally organised, social form or practices which are seen as necessary for, or at least contributing to, such a life.[10] Thus morality involves not so much a set of constraints on individuals' actions, but a positive vision of the human good; and moral philosophy is inherently social philosophy.

Both Marx's work, and much of the socialist tradition generally, may reasonably be located within this Aristotelian framework. Yet both have often been criticised for the unduly monolithic nature of their social vision, for seeing the human good as realisable within a single ideal form of social practices and institutions. I shall say more about this criticism later. But I regard it as a virtue of Walzer's position, to which I now turn, that it is based on a strongly pluralistic conception of the human good, and thus

---

[8] Cf. Raymond Plant, 'Enterprise in its Place: the Moral Limits of Markets', in Paul Heelas and Paul Morris, eds., *The Values of the Enterprise Culture*, Routledge, London, 1992, pp. 85–99.

[9] See Russell Keat and Nicholas Abercrombie, eds., *Enterprise Culture*, Routledge, London, 1991.

[10] See Alasdair MacIntyre, *After Virtue*, Duckworth, London, 1981; Joseph Raz, *The Morality of Freedom*, Oxford University Press, Oxford, 1985; William Kymlicka, *Liberalism, Community and Culture*, Oxford University Press, Oxford, 1989; and John O'Neill, *Ecology, Policy and Politics: Human Well-Being and the Natural World*, Routledge, London, forthcoming.

also emphasises the need to construct boundaries around the various institutional contexts—including that of the market—in which diverse and distinctive social practices can flourish.[11]

Walzer and the separation of spheres

Walzer's discussion of market boundaries forms part of a more general account of the nature of social justice in modern societies. He takes it to be a characteristic (perhaps defining) feature of such societies that they involve a high degree of differentiation between various domains or spheres within which distinctive kinds of social activities take place: the economy, politics, the family, education, welfare, religion, etc. Each of these spheres involves different forms of social relationships, different criteria of permissible and impermissible actions, and different rules of distribution for the specific 'social goods' with which they are concerned: e.g. money and wealth, political power and office, love and friendship, knowledge and expertise, health and security, religious salvation.[12]

Walzer maintains that it is precisely the specificity—or, as he terms it, the 'plurality'—of these social goods (which themselves also vary between different societies at different times) that makes it impossible to defend principles of distributive justice of the kind standardly proposed by political philosophers, whether these are egalitarian, desert-based, Rawlsian, Nozickian or otherwise. For these typically involve either mistakenly assuming that all such goods are somehow commensurable with one another (e.g. that they are different ways of achieving the single good of utility, or even measurable in monetary terms), or attempting to apply to every social good a principle that is in fact appropriate only to some.

Any adequate theory of justice must therefore recognise the essential plurality and incommensurability of social goods and their specific meanings; and this Walzer attempts in his own account. The requirements of social justice are twofold. First, within each sphere social goods must be distributed in accordance with the criteria appropriate to those goods— criteria which are implicit in what he terms their 'social meanings'. Secondly, and more importantly in his view, each sphere must be prevented from 'colonizing' others: in particular, people's success in one sphere must be prevented from enabling them to achieve corresponding success in another, despite their lacking the attributes that would justify

[11] 'Pluralism' here, as throughout, means the existence of a number of distinct—and probably incommensurable—kinds of 'good', all of which may contribute to people's well-being. It thus differs from other current senses of the term, e.g. the presence of a single society/nation of various social/cultural groups which differ radically in their values, beliefs etc.

[12] Walzer's mapping of social goods onto specific spheres is at times haphazard; and some social goods, e.g. honour, recognition and respect, seem to be involved in several spheres. I shall ignore these problems.

9

such success according to the criteria regarded as appropriate in that other sphere.

What I have here termed 'colonization' involves what Walzer himself refers to as 'dominance': 'I call a good dominant if the individuals who have it, because they have it, can command a wide range of other goods' (p. 10). Examples of dominance include 'nepotism'—the illicit colonization of the economy by the sphere of the family/kinship relations; and the use of wealth to gain political power or office—the illicit colonization of the political sphere by that of the economy.[13]

Walzer regards the (market) economy, or what he terms 'the sphere of money and commodities', as the most dangerous potential (and actual) colonizer in modern societies. As he puts it at one point, in a way that should give pause for thought to those enthusiasts for the market who see it as the main bulwark against totalitarian dominance by the state:

> One can conceive of the market [if one is not careful, that is] as a sphere without boundaries, an unzoned city—for money is insidious, and market relations are expansive. A radically *laissez-faire* economy would be like a totalitarian state, invading every other sphere, dominating every other distributive process. It would transform every social good into a commodity. This is market imperialism.[14]

He thus devotes much attention to how the market's imperialistic or colonizing tendencies are and can be controlled. Part of his solution I shall not discuss here: it concerns the internal organisation of large-scale capitalist firms which, he argues, should be reconstructed as co-operatively owned and controlled 'socialist' enterprises so as to prevent economic power illicitly being translated into political power at the micro-level.

The other part consists in specifying a series of what he calls 'blocked exchanges'—prohibitions on the sale and purchase of various goods, which are intended to limit the market's dominating tendencies, and thus to 'separate', to mark out the boundaries of, the economic sphere. On Walzer's strikingly heterogeneous list of blocked exchanges one finds the following items: human beings themselves; divine grace (c.f. the sin of simony); political influence, votes and office; prizes, honours and all outcomes of verdicts based on criteria of desert; marriage partners, love and friendship; harmful or dangerous goods and services such as drugs and homicide; and several others.[15]

[13] Notice that the very idea of nepotism as a vice is perhaps a distinctively 'modern' one, presupposing a separation of kinship from other spheres, absent in many pre-modern societies. This may cast some light on the ambivalent attitudes towards nepotism that some commentators detect in Japanese politics.

[14] *Op. cit.*, pp. 119–120. Walzer correspondingly sees a central role of the state as the maintenance of boundaries between other spheres, and is sensitive to the problems of how this can be done without the state itself colonizing them: see especially Chapter 12.

[15] Walzer's list is intended to represent what are currently regarded as blocked exchanges in the USA and similar societies. For a recent discussion of various possible rationales for disallowing such exchanges, see Judith Andre, 'Blocked Exchanges: A Taxonomy', *Ethics*, vol. 103, 1992, pp 29–47.

10

But Walzer is aware that even if these blocked exchanges are success-fully enforced—which is itself no mean task—this may well not ensure their primary objective, the prevention of market dominance. For example, even if political office cannot directly be bought, it may as it were be indirectly purchased, through the undue influence of wealth or economic power on the outcome of political processes. Walzer proposes a number of measures that might prevent such injustices; but I shall not discuss these here.

Instead, I want to suggest that there is an important dimension of market colonization which Walzer's pluralistic conception of social goods and institutional spheres potentially enables one to discern, but which he himself tends to ignore—perhaps because of his relatively narrow focus on questions of distributive justice. To introduce this further dimension of the boundary problem, I shall first comment on the relationship between Walzer's pluralism and some central themes in the work of Marx and Hegel.

Marx, Hegel and the separation of spheres

In an article published shortly after the appearance of *Spheres of Justice*,[16] Walzer notes how unconvincing, and indeed unattractive, his position will appear to those who endorse certain key features of Marx's thought. On the one hand, the very idea of separating and limiting the sphere of the market may seem absurd in the light of even quite modest versions of historical materialism—of overall determination by the economy of the character of other social domains. And on the other, his pluralistic account of the good society—which includes, *inter alia*, the sphere of the market—seems clearly at odds with Marx's vision of communist society, which not only leaves no place for the market, but is also, at least arguably, essentially non-pluralistic in its ideal conception of social relationships.

For example, when Marx argued in his essay 'On the Jewish Question' that human emancipation requires overcoming the separation between civil society (a market economy) and the state (liberal-democratic political institutions), he seemed to imply that both political and economic life should ideally be conducted on the same basis, displaying similar kinds of social relations, attitudes, motivations, values, and so on. Thus, in particular, truly human production is an activity in which humans self-consciously aim to satisfy one another's needs, and to realise a common good; and it is conducted in that same co-operative and communal manner that also characterises, at least in theory, a democratic political system. By contrast, of course, market-governed production represents the very antithesis of such social relationships.[17]

[16] 'Liberalism and the Art of Separation', *Political Theory*, vol. 12, 1984, pp. 315–30.
[17] Here I rely on the interpretation of Marx's essay proposed in my 'Liberal Rights and Socialism', in Keith Graham, ed., *Contemporary Political Philosophy*, Cambridge University Press, Cambridge, 1982, pp. 59–82.

11

In these respects Marx's position differs crucially from that of Hegel, whose well-known trio of family, state and civil society is much closer in spirit to Walzer's pluralism. For each of Hegel's 'spheres' involves its own specific forms of social relationships, attitudes and values; and all of these—albeit also through their dialectical relations with one another—are seen as positive and indeed necessary features of the good society.

In particular, this applies to the individualistic, contractual relations of exchange involved in one key element of Hegel's 'civil society', the economic market, despite his evident concern that some of the latter's potential effects should be held in check by other elements, including both 'corporations' and the system of welfare. But Hegel is even more concerned that the model of contractual exchange—which has a quite proper role in the economic domain—should not be allowed to distort or undermine the quite different kinds of relationships involved in other spheres, including that of marriage and the family.[18] In this respect, he can be seen as recognising precisely that dimension of potential market colonization that, as I shall argue shortly, needs to be added to Walzer's account.

But how might the viability—as distinct from the desirability—of this pluralistic ideal be affected by Marx's historical materalism? Would not the latter, if true, make the idea of limiting the dominance of the market absurdly unrealistic? Here I want to suggest that even if the character of the economic domain does (broadly) determine that of others, this is not necessarily damaging to Walzer's 'Hegelian' separation of spheres. For such determination might take either of two distinct forms, which I shall call 'replicatory' and 'non-replicatory'; and it is only the former that would be clearly problematic.

Replicatory determination would involve the specific character of, e.g. market relations, being 'projected' upon other domains. In Marx's own work perhaps the classic example of this form of historical materialism is found in his remarks about Utilitarianism in *The German Ideology*. Here he claims that the apparent plausibility of what is assumed by this theory, i.e. the possibility of comparing all human actions in terms of the amounts of utility they generate, itself results from the projection onto all forms of social activity the character of exchange relations in the economic market—a generalised 'commodification' of social life stemming from the market's colonizing powers.

But elsewhere in Marx's work, and in that of later Marxist theorists, one also finds examples of the non-replicatory form of historical materialism. Consider, for instance, the claim that the rise of the market has brought with it the creation of a particular form of family life, one in which personal intimacy, romantic love and emotional intensity predominate. Here it is precisely the dissimilarity of market and personal relations that is emphasised; and this may be explained, in a broadly functionalist manner,

---

[18] G. W. F. Hegel, *The Philosophy of Right*, trans. T. M. Knox, Clarendon Press, Oxford, 1952: Third Part, especially paras 158–69.

12

by reference to the need for some 'haven' in the 'heartless world' of economic life if the economy is itself to operate successfully.[19] Whether or not such explanations are correct, they seem both consistent with historical materialism, and to show the possible consistency of this with Walzerian separation.

Markets and commodities, literal and non-literal

Returning now to Walzer, and drawing implicitly on this brief discussion of Marx and Hegel, I shall make two sets of comments about his account of blocked exchanges which are intended to indicate what is missing in the way he conceptualises the problem of market boundaries.

The first concerns the relationship between markets and commodities. Walzer tends to identify the sphere of the market with that of money and commodities, themselves defined as things that can be bought and sold. Yet the question of what we regard as legitimately bought and sold is by no means the same as what we regard as legitimately produced and distributed specifically through the mechanisms of a market economy. (Indeed, in light of recent experience with the European exchange rate mechanism, some might like to protect money itself from the market!) For example, blood may be bought and sold in a centralised state-controlled economy; and whatever arguments there are against this will thus apply to both state and market economies.

Taking this point a little further one might suggest that, somewhat paradoxically, many of the blocked exchanges that Walzer draws to our attention have themselves, historically, been associated with the rise of the market as the primary means of economic organisation; and hence—if one accepts Polanyi's influential thesis—with the very emergence of a 'separate' (in his terms 'disembedded') economic sphere.[20] Indeed, this historical process of 'separation' may itself have been linked to significant limitations on at least some of 'the things that money could buy' in pre-market societies.

But whether or not this last speculation is correct, it at least seems clear that if one's concern is with the boundaries of the market domain, an exclusive focus on what can properly be bought and sold may well not fully capture what is at issue, and may even be misleading. For example, any worries that one might have about the extension of the market to include higher education are unlikely to be confined to the possibility of qualifications such as university degrees becoming straightforwardly purchasable. They will additionally, and perhaps more significantly, be directed at the possible effects of market forces on the character of educational

---

[19] For discussion of this, and especially its implications for gender relations, see Ross Poole, *Morality and Modernity*, Routledge, London, 1991.

[20] See Karl Polanyi, *The Great Transformation*, Rinehart, New York, 1944.

institutions themselves, on the kinds of commitments and attitudes that may be encouraged in their participants, and so on.

My second set of comments concern what is meant by the term 'commodity' itself. If one considers Walzer's list of blocked exchanges one can, I think, distinguish two kinds of cases. First, there are those where the item could, as it were, perfectly well be bought and sold (and/or provided through the market), but where one has reasons either for not allowing this, or for also securing provision through non-market means—for example, dangerous or harmful goods; or bodily organs, health-care, etc. Secondly, there are those where one feels that the item concerned just cannot be purchased, or at least not without radically transforming or devaluing its existing or desired character—for example, love and friendship, 'things' which, it is often said, 'money can't buy', and which are devalued when any attempt to do so is made.

However, if one considers why one believes that these latter kinds of items 'cannot' be bought or sold one will, I suggest, need to focus not so much on the purely formal/legal fact of their being 'purchased', but rather on what might be called the social meaning (or perhaps meanings) of such transactions—to what is involved in treating or regarding something **as** a commodity. Once this is recognised, one will also realise that things (including people) may be treated or regarded in this way without literally becoming commodities, in the sense of formally purchasable items; and indeed that it is the former, rather than the latter, that is the morally significant feature here.

Thus, being literally a commodity is not a necessary condition for being regarded as one in the morally relevant sense—and indeed it is quite possibly not a sufficient condition either, though I shall not pursue this point. Correspondingly, a system of blocked exchanges, however successful, may still prove seriously inadequate in preventing the colonizing tendencies of the sphere of commodities.[21]

At this point what is needed is some substantive account of the social meaning(s) of 'commodities'. One such account has been provided in a recent article by Elizabeth Anderson.[22] She suggests that the meaning of commodities should be understood primarily in terms of how they are valued by people: for their use to their possessor (and in particular for their ability to satisfy their possessor's desires or preferences) rather than for any intrinsic value of their own; in impersonal ways which make them exchangeable with, or replaceable by, others, that are seen as commensurable with them; and as exclusive rather than shared goods—ones whose

---

[21] Note that the problem here is not the previously mentioned one that money may indirectly buy access to inappropriately purchased items, but that such items may inappropriately be 'thought of' in the way that purchasable items are. An example of this is perhaps unwittingly provided by Walzer's own account of the social good of 'recognition': *op. cit.*, pp. 249–59.

[22] 'The Ethical Limitations of the Market', *Economics and Philosophy*, vol. 6, 1990, pp. 179–206.

enjoyment by someone excludes, rather than depends on, their also being enjoyed by others.

Anderson goes on to show in some detail how the process of com-modification, defined in this way, is destructive of the kinds of relation-ships and activities involved in the 'personal' sphere of love and friendship, of the family, and so on. But I shall not pursue this: instead, I shall draw together the preceding comments about the limitations of Walzer's account of blocked exchanges, and consider briefly their implications for boundaries between the market and the political domain.[23] I shall then go on to discuss the kinds of cultural institutions and practices referred to at the outset, which cannot be seen as belonging to either the personal or political spheres, yet may likewise need protection from the colonizing tendencies of the market.

Political judgments and market preferences

If one accepts that the market domain is not merely that of commodities, in the sense of what can be purchased; and that commodities themselves are not merely what can be purchased, but also what is socially 'meant' by this; then one must also accept that the dominance of the market domain might itself take the form of an illegitimate extension of its social meanings and norms to other institutions and activities, without these being straight-forwardly (re-) located within the market. The political sphere provides ample illustrations of such potential (and indeed actual) forms of coloniza-tion. I will focus briefly on just one, whose significance has emerged in recent discussions of environmental decision-making, but whose implica-tions go well beyond this particular context.

An increasingly influential approach to environmental decision-making has been to employ an extended version of standard forms of cost-benefit analysis—extended, in particular, so as to include in its calculations some measurement of the value that people attribute to features of the environ-ment through their hypothetical 'willingness-to-pay' for them, or 'to-be-compensated' for their removal. But, as Mark Sagoff has recently argued, this approach involves an illicit transformation of political decisions into analogues of market decisions.[24] That is, although recourse to the tech-niques of cost-benefit analysis is typically made precisely where the straightforward use of market mechanisms is thought to be inadequate— i.e. in cases of 'market failure'—it is Sagoff's view that these techniques nonetheless preserve certain basic features of the market which are

---

[23] Anderson also considers commodification in the political domain; but whereas her account emphasises the contrast between preferences and needs, mine will focus on that between preferences and judgments.

[24] In *The Economy of the Earth*, Cambridge University Press, Cambridge, 1988. Cf. John Elster, 'The Market and the Forum', in J. Elster and A. Hylland, *Foundations of Social Choice Theory*, Cambridge University Press, Cambridge, 1986; and John O'Neill, *op. cit.*

15

inappropriate to decisions that should instead be made politically, and indeed democratically.

One crucial element in this illicit transformation is, he suggests, the assimilation of what should be regarded as judgments of value to what are 'no more than' the expression of individual preferences: i.e. to those rather mysterious entities which—at least in neo-classical economic theory—are indicated by a consumer's willingness to purchase something, and whose 'satisfaction' the market is supposedly so efficient in achieving. And certainly it is a central feature of the market that consumer preferences require no justification, no basis in defensible judgments, for them to be 'permitted' to affect what is produced—a feature which is reflected in the insistent agnosticism of neo-classical theorists about the desirability or otherwise of such preferences.[25]

By contrast, claims Sagoff, neither judgments of value in general, nor political judgments in particular, should be understood as the expression of preferences. Instead they should be seen as attempts to make justifiable claims about 'the good' (in the case of politics, the common good), stemming from reflective processes and open to critical evaluation, debate and so on. And since this is so, the reduction of political decision-making to a technique for the satisfaction of preferences, 'taken as given and beyond the bounds of critical debate', must be resisted. It would, in effect, be to confuse what Sagoff regards as the entirely distinct social meanings of people's roles as citizens and as consumers, and thus to transgress the boundaries between politics and the market.[26]

The domain of cultural practices

Whatever the merits of Sagoff's specific claims about environmental decisions, his argument nicely illustrates some of the issues involved in thinking about market boundaries if one conceives of separation and colonization in the ways I have suggested. I shall now take these further by considering their possible application to the kinds of cultural practices and institutions noted earlier—to broadcasting, sports, academic research, journalism, the various arts (whether 'high' or 'popular'), and so on.

The proper place for these in relation to the market sphere is, I think, much more difficult to determine for whereas there would be widespread agreement about the need for boundaries between the market and the domains of personal and political life—even if there is disagreement about

[25] For further discussion of the neo-classical conception of preferences, see my 'Scepticism, Authority and the Market', in Russell Keat, Nigel Whiteley and Nicholas Abercrombie, eds., *The Authority of the Consumer*, Routledge, London, forthcoming.

[26] This is by no means the only example of such colonization: similar issues are raised in e.g. the displacement of political argument by the techniques of market research and advertising.

precisely why this is so, and how such boundaries can in practice be maintained—there is much less agreement in the case of these activities. I shall begin by indicating a number of features that, at least in their ideal form, they may have in common.

I take as my starting-point two central elements in Alasdair MacIntyre's account of what he refers to, in his own philosophically specific sense of the term, as a (social) practice:[27]

(i) Any cultural practice involves a set of standards or criteria which serve to identify what counts as a good or bad, exemplary or worthless, competent or incompetent instance of the activity concerned, and by reference to which the merits of particular attempts to achieve the practice's overall aims or goals are to be judged. Its participants must thus be willing, at least initially—for these standards are not sacrosanct or unchangeable—to subordinate their individual judgments and preferences to the authority of the practice's own criteria; and

(ii) Only by doing so can they come to appreciate and enjoy what MacIntyre terms the internal goods of the practice—such as the elegance of a scientific theory, the truthfulness of a theatrical performance, or the brilliance of a sequence of passes in a game of football. The nature of these goods can be understood only in relation to the specific character of the practice concerned; and in this, amongst other respects, they differ from what he terms external goods, the primary examples of which are money, power and prestige.

I will now elaborate and develop this account in ways that are intended, *inter alia*, implicitly to suggest how cultural practices differ from the two non-market domains of personal and political life considered earlier.

(iii) Amongst the primary motivations of those who participate in any cultural practice is their enjoyment of its internal goods and, more generally, of their acquisition and exercise of the various skills and capacities which its standards both make possible and require. By contrast, the pursuit of external goods, whilst by no means necessarily absent, must not come to predominate, especially if this leads to actions that are at odds with the practice's internal goals and standards. Hence financial rewards, in particular, should function mainly as material forms of deserved recognition for practice-defined contributions—as goods whose absence may cause resentment rather than as primary motivators.

(iv) Cultural practices typically involve some broad division between, as it were, 'performers' and 'audiences'. I use these terms in rather extended senses, to refer to distinctions such as those between writers and readers, players and spectators, broadcasters and viewers, curators and visitors.[28] Typically the 'performance' of a practice's activities is seen as

[27] MacIntyre, *op. cit.*, especially ch.14, p. 175.
[28] I ignore here the many divisions within the category of 'performers' (and indeed of 'audiences'), which are often of considerable significance—e.g. between actors, playwrights, directors and producers in the case of theatre. A similar point applies to the distinction between 'producers' and 'consumers' in a market economy.

17

radically incomplete, as less valuable or successful, in the absence of such audiences—whose members may themselves at least partly share the kinds of enjoyment of the practice's internal goods that are experienced by performers.

(v) But this is not to say that performers are primarily concerned to promote the well-being of their audiences by providing them with the opportunity to enjoy the practice's internal goods. They are not, that is, altruistic in this respect; nor in their primary motivation for engagement in the practice. Neither do they (need to) see themselves as aiming to realise 'the common good'. Nonetheless, they may well be inclined to think there is something worthwhile, pleasurable, valuable etc. about what their practices 'produce'; and because they believe this—believe, as it were, in the practice—they may hope that their audiences will think or come to think likewise.

(vi) Relatedly, both performers and audiences are likely to form various kinds and degree of attachment to these practices and their 'products'. Such attachments may often involve admiration, respect etc. for particular individuals who are seen as exemplary of the practice concerned, or as contributing to its development and flourishing. But such attachments are often also to 'the practices themselves'—to music, football, athletics, literature—rather than to particular individuals. Nor should these attachments—which may range from 'interest in', through 'concern for', to 'love of'—be understood as requiring participants to see the practice as an essential element of their own, individual identities.[29]

(vii) Finally, it would be misleading to represent a cultural practice's participants as necessarily involved in a self-consciously co-operative or collective project—in the way that, e.g., political activity is often depicted by radical democrats. Certainly the internal goods of a practice are at least potentially 'shared' rather than 'exclusive' ones (cf Anderson's definition of commodities, above); and also, as already indicated, participants will tend to recognise their dependence upon, and enrichment by, the efforts and contributions of others. But the kinds of bonds that may be generated by this are, as it were, mediated by the practice itself, and are also quite compatible with various forms and degrees of competition, rivalry and the like between its participants.

Markets and practices

Given this highly schematic account of the nature of cultural practices, one can then consider the question of how far, and for what reasons, their existence might be vulnerable to colonization by the market—to the kinds

[29] Here I want to resist the tendency amongst recent 'communitarian' philosophers to espouse a re-socialisation of individual identity. My own account is intended to be consistent with certain versions of liberal 'individualism' (as in Kymlicka, and Raz, *op. cit.*): the best forms of attachment are, I believe, formed by individuals with clear 'boundaries' around them.

of processes that people frequently object to when they criticise, e.g., the 'commercialisation of sports', the de-regulation of broadcasting, or the introduction of new forms of intellectual property in academic research.

I shall present a quite brief, and deliberately hypothetical answer to this question: the subordination of such practices to the market is at least potentially damaging to them **if** one accepts something like the standard account of the market provided by neo-classical economic theorists.

The first argument invokes the concept of consumer sovereignty, according to which the operation of the market involves the control of producer-decisions by consumer-preferences. But there is no guarantee that such preferences will be informed by or in any way respect the 'authority' of the goals and standards of the practice concerned: the market refuses to discriminate between preferences, whereas practices insist on doing so. Any particular group of 'marketised' cultural practitioners is thus highly vulnerable to competition from rival 'producers' who are willing and able to cater, more profitably, for consumers whose preferences may be entirely antithetical to the meaning and standards of the practice concerned.

The second argument concerns the respective roles of internal and external goods. Market activities are oriented to the competitive acquisition of external goods. Thus the participants in a market-governed practice will treat it primarily as a means of acquiring such goods, regarding its internal goods as of relatively little significance. Whilst it is possible that the actions resulting from these different motivations will at times coincide, it is equally possible that they will not; and when the latter situation obtains, the 'logic of the market' dictates which will be performed. The outcome will tend to be damaging to the integrity of the practice, given the close connection between the nature of its internal goods, the maintenance of its standards, and the effective pursuit of its goals. Such damaging outcomes can be avoided only if the practice's members altruistically resist the logic of the market, being willing actually to sacrifice their interest in external goods rather than merely being relatively unconcerned with them.[30]

But suppose instead that the neo-classical account of market economies is mistaken, or seriously flawed. Then, not only might these kinds of arguments for the exclusion of cultural practices from the market domain lose some of their force, it might even turn out that economic activities conducted within that domain could themselves display at least some of the features that I have ascribed to (cultural) practices. And if, as I would argue, engagement in such practices is itself a significant element in human well-being, in the realisation of 'the human good', then perhaps there are

---

[30] See John O'Neill, 'Altruism, Egoism and the Market', *The Philosophical Forum*, vol. XXIII, 1992, pp. 278–288. For a more detailed presentation of these two arguments, see my 'Consume Sovereignty and the Integrity of Practices', in Keat and Abercrombie, eds., *op. cit.*, pp. 216–30.

19

particular forms of a market economy that at least come closer than others to enabling such practice-dependent well-being to be realised.

At this point, what I have said in this paper might begin to engage more directly with some of the themes that are addressed in other contributions to this volume. For example, perhaps some of the 'varieties of capitalism' are ones in which, as it were, businesses are conducted as practices. And certainly I am often struck by the ways in which, for example, ICI's recent defence against a take-over bid from the 'predatory' Hanson, or Granada TV's opposition to the de-regulation of broadcasting, sound so similar to the opposition of academics to the commercialisation of their institutions, or of subsidised theatre companies to the kinds of business plans and marketing strategies foisted upon them by the Arts Council.[31]

But I will end on a cautionary note. There is a danger here of being seduced by a particular kind of optimism: the optimism of believing that capitalism works best, most effectively, when it also works in a way that is most 'morally desirable'—far less brutishly and nastily than the neo-classical picture suggests. Co-operation, education, concern for long-term consequences: how admirable these are—and how fortunate that they are just what the effective operation of capitalism requires anyway! It would be nice if this were so, but I doubt that it can altogether be justified. In the case of competition v. co-operation, for example, any one commercial enterprise may well depend for its success on co-operation between its managers and workers, and even with its suppliers. But it is still engaged in a competitive struggle with other firms; and even if this is mitigated by further co-operation at the level of the nation-state, this itself may be required only to give that nation a competitive advantage over others.

---

[31] Notice here that when commercial forms of organisation, and/or market mechanisms, are introduced into public sector services through government policy, they typically express that government's conception of how the private sector and/or the market actually or best operates. In the UK, this has mainly been based on highly disputable and ideologically inspired versions of neo-classical theory.

THE NEW POLITICS OF ECONOMICS

DAVID MILIBAND*

In the last twenty years, the withering of the welfare state consensus in Western Europe and the collapse of communist government in the Eastern bloc have undermined important assumptions, perhaps illusions, of socialist and social democratic politics. In some quarters, these twin developments have been interpreted not just as a triumph of free market economics, but also as final proof of its symbiotic relationship with liberal democracy: Francis Fukuyama's (in)famous article 'The End of History' and his subsequent book are only the most articulate examples of this thesis.[1]

An indication of the strength of the new hegemony comes, ironically enough, from the Fabian Society, whose founding premise 100 years ago was that the intervention of the expert state could remedy the market failures of Victorian capitalism. The Society's first post-election pamphlet in 1992, *The Name of the Rose*, by David Lipsey, argued that the Labour Party should no longer see the debate about economic policy as an 'ideological battleground'. It repeats a familiar litany: government intervention causes lower growth, lower investment, lower employment—'that is how a market economy is', as Lipsey puts it.[2]

I want to suggest, to the contrary, that to learn from the failures of command economics on the one hand and the limitations of Keynesian social democracy on the other does not require the abandonment of political designs on economic futures. The near-universal acceptance of the power of markets in a mixed economy need not entail a new economic consensus, nor the end of ambitions for economic change. To tap the potential of *a* market economy does not mean acceptance of *this* one.

The context

In their own way, and in particular historical circumstances, each of the three governing ideologies of the twentieth century—broadly speaking command communism, Keynesian social democracy, and revived neoliberalism—provided coherent explanatory narratives for the shape of the (economic) world and for its reform. But though central planning

* David Miliband is Research Fellow at the Institute for Public Policy Research and Secretary of the Commission on Social Justice. This paper develops one theme of the IPPR publication *Next Left: An Agenda for the 1990s*, IPPR, London, 1992.

[1] Francis Fukuyama, *The End of History and the Last Man*, Macmillan, London, 1991.
[2] David Lipsey, *The Name of the Rose*, Fabian Society, London, 1992.

promised an end to economic waste and distributional conflict, it fuelled one and only suppressed the other. Keynesian demand management vowed to smooth the business cycle, but was left impotent in the face of 1970s stagflation. And although neoliberalism promised to spur economic growth through a combination of monetary control, tax cuts and deregulation, it has instead induced bankruptcy, debt and recession where it has been most vigorously pursued.

In the countries of Western Europe and Scandinavia what has been called 'Keynesian Social Democracy' or the 'Keynesian Welfare State' provided in the wake of the Great Depression an intellectually coherent and politically compelling alternative to the injustice and inefficiency of inter-war *laissez-faire*. During its 'golden age' after 1945, what was loosely a social democratic compromise combined in advanced capitalist countries high rates of growth with the extension of social rights and the gradual diminution of economic inequality. The central axioms of the post-war settlement—cross-party commitments to full employment, a mixed economy, and universal welfare and education services— established during the 1950s in Britain and Western Europe more generally an intellectual hegemony as strong as the neoclassical orthodoxy of the 1920s.

In Britain, the traditions and practice of labourism—epitomised by sectional trade unionism, Fabian gradualism and welfare paternalism— had long been attacked from the Marxist left for its weakness and contradictions, and from the new left by the challenge of anti-statist, feminist and ecological politics. It was on the Right, however, that the post-war settlement met its nemesis. The fiscal and political crises of the 'entitlement state', crises symbolised for Robert Kuttner by the burgeoning revolt against increased tax burdens, and diminished faith in the state as an agency of good works,[3] ushered in a neo-liberal counter-revolution, committed above all to rolling back state intervention in economic affairs. Ideas that in the 1960s were confined to a laager of neo-liberal true believers came in the 1980s to dominate policy development. Longstanding goals of *laissez-faire* purists, for example the privatisation of money to control inflation,[4] continue to have minority appeal, but the avowed *Weltanschauung* of the leading British neo-liberal 'think-tank', the Institute of Economic Affairs, namely scepticism of the economic performance of the state, became widely shared.

With remarkable speed, however, the neo-liberal project seems to have run once again into intellectual and political trouble. Social polarisation, far from spurring economic efficiency, has gone hand in hand with deep and wounding recession. Deregulation, for instance in financial services, has sponsored a debilitating cycle of boom and bust. And the systematic rejection of any notion of the public interest—in education and training,

[3] Robert Kuttner, *The Economic Illusion: False Choices between Prosperity and Social Justice*, University of Pennsylvania Press, Philadelphia, 1984.
[4] See Arthur Seldon, *Capitalism*, Blackwell, Oxford, 1990.

research and development, or physical infrastructure—has enfeebled growth potential.

In the current context, however, a swing of the pendulum back towards the *status quo ante* seems inadequate, both as analysis and prescription. The simplistic dualisms of the last decade, public versus private, collective versus individual, state versus market, do not do justice either to the differences that already exist between the mixed economies of advanced capitalism, or to the economic, social and environmental choices we face.

The politics of economics

The terms of economic debate—from the microeconomics of competitive markets to the macroeconomics of unemployment and inflation—have been defined on narrow neoclassical terms since the 1970s. A model of independent, self-regulating markets, free of the dead hand of political intervention, has been dominant. In Britain, as John Gray has written, '(T)he chief success of Thatcherism . . . is in the decoupling of the fortunes of the economy from the performance of government . . . by creating the perception of the autonomy of market institutions'.[5]

Laissez-faire partisans have claimed that the market is a neutral and beneficient institution, saved by the spur of competition from the in-efficiencies of the public sector. They promised that conflicts of interest would be resolved by the neutral arbitration of the 'colour-blind and accent-deaf' market.[6] They insisted above all that no one—certainly no politician—could be held responsible for market outcomes. This was the animating theme drawn from the work of Friedrich Hayek. He maintained that market processes, made up of millions of individual decisions, 'can be neither just nor unjust, because the results are not intended or foreseen, and depend on a multitude of circumstances not known in their totality to anybody'.[7]

In this model, markets and the economic systems they make up are sovereign and self-equilibrating mechanisms, driven by the utility-maximising, rational, and self-interested motives of independent actors in the marketplace. All commodities are bought and sold in markets of many sellers and a multiplicity of buyers, with price movements regulating the system and bringing supply and demand into harmony. Shocks to one part of the system are accommodated elsewhere, by changes in price. As Fred Block writes, 'self-regulation makes the economy a seamless web'.[8]

Each privatisation, deregulation, and tax cut of the last decade has been premised on simple principles, highlighted by Fritz Scharpf: '(1) that all markets tend to equilibrium; (2) that in equilibrium all productive

[5] John Gray, 'Enlightenment projects' in *Times Literary Supplement*, 14 August 1992.

[6] Seldon, *op. cit.*

[7] Quoted in Desmond King, *The New Right: Politics, Markets and Citizenship*, Macmillan, London, 1987.

[8] Fred Block, *Post-Industrial Possibilities*, California University Press, Berkeley, 1990.

23

opportunities are exploited, all job seekers are employed, and all realisable consumer demands are met; and (3) that actual markets will approximate to equilibrium conditions when a workable degree of competition and flexible prices are assured.[9] Three assertions have been central to policy prescriptions: first, the insistence that markets exist antecedent of society; second, and consequently, that they are governed by unchanging rules, whatever the context; and third, that political intervention and market efficiency are locked in a zero-sum game, more of one implying less of the other.

David Marquand has pointed out that the (first) claim of market primacy goes to the heart of British political culture, suffused as it is 'with the values and assumptions of Whiggery, above all with the central Lockean assumption that individual property rights are antecedent to society'.[10] Collective action is held not simply to be an intrusion on individual freedom but a subversion of pre-existing market rationality.

The problem is that there is no evidence for the assertion that collectivities and collective action are secondary phenomena, either for individuals—in what Etzioni describes as the 'undersocialised' Lockean sense that they represent merely the delegated sovereignty of atomised individuals, or the 'oversocialised' Hobbesian conception of the controlling state—or for markets, in their relations with society at large. Just as Etzioni asserts that 'individuals and communities are both completely essential, and hence have the same fundamental standing',[11] so markets and the state not only co-exist, but stand interdependent. As Moran and Wright have said, 'the state is needed to manage the inputs to markets, the terms on which exchanges are made and the outputs and impacts of those exchanges';[12] or as Raymond Plant puts it, 'the intellectual debate since Reagan, Thatcher and the changes in Eastern Europe ... (is) about the range of social and political institutions in which markets are embedded, the scope and purposes of these institutions ... along with the debate about the scope of the market and the range of goods which ought to be treated as commodities'.[13]

In other words, in the process of their interaction, market and state construct and reform each other. In place of the static allocative assumptions of the equilibrium model there is here an emphasis on the dynamic interdependence between markets and the societies in which they are located. In the case of the labour market, the interaction of the welfare

[9] Fritz Scharpf, *Crisis and Choice in European Social Democracy*, Cornell University Press, Ithaca, 1991, p. 20.

[10] David Marquand, *The Unprincipled Society*, Fontana, London, 1988, p. 154.

[11] Amitai Etzioni, *The Moral Dimension: Towards a New Economics*, Free Press, New York, 1988, p. 8.

[12] Michael Moran and Maurice Wright, 'The Interdependence of Markets and States' in Moran and Wright, eds., *The Market and the State: Studies in Interdependence*, Macmillan, Basingstoke, 1991, p. 244.

[13] Raymond Plant, 'Autonomy, Social Rights and Distributive Justice', in John Gray, *The Moral Foundations of Market Institutions*, IEA, London, 1992, p. 119.

state—in its broadest sense, from levels of unemployment benefit to the tax treatment of married women's income—with employer demands and social mores drive the employment structure. Far from being 'natural', markets are political.

The second claim under review is that a market logic exists independent of social conditions, more or less fettered by the interference of the state, but regulated by the relentless drive of human nature and competitive advantage. As World Bank Chief Economist Lawrence Summers put it in 1991: 'Spread the truth—the laws of economics are like the laws of engineering. One set of laws works everywhere.'[14] In this model, economy and society are set up as completely separate spheres.

The problem with such a separation—it is almost too obvious to state— is that not only do economic choices severely constrain social ambitions, but social context shapes the logic of market outcomes. On the one hand, 'voluntarist' deregulated economies, representing one type of market-state relation, eat away at attempts to mitigate their worst features precisely because they are driven by a logic—created, not natural—of vast income disparities, a large population of unemployed 'outsiders', and a chronic tendency to boom and bust. On the other hand, at a minimum, an alternative market structure is evident in economies with thick networks of collective intervention and regulation, where the infrastructure of local government, trade unions, trade associations and Chambers of Commerce combine with nationally-regulated labour and product markets to impose a different logic on market operations, promoting competition in quality rather than price, collaboration to meet common needs, and investment in the whole population rather than part of it.

The (third) neo-liberal claim is of a zero-sum game between a political sphere based on and concerned with equity and a market sphere concerned with efficiency. In Britain, this competitive game was symbolised by the establishment of nationalisation and privatisation as the poles of political debate.[15] On a unilinear spectrum stretching from command economics at one end to perfect competition at the other, any increase in state intervention was assumed to decrease market power.

Today, however, individual economies are not simply distinctive for the place they occupy on this unilinear spectrum. The new mixed economy is more than a compromise between the extremes of command communism and *laissez faire*. As we will discuss below, each mixed economy, and each part of each mixed economy, has its own logic, institutions and character based on a complex interdependence of state, market and citizen at local, regional and national level. The point is not simply that regulation can serve to increase competition, though this is of course true. More important regulation or collective intervention of any kind *changes*

[14] Quoted in William Keegan, *The Spectre of Capitalism*, Radius, London, 1992, p. 109.
[15] Ben Pimlott quotes Aneurin Bevan as saying that 'the only difference between us and the Tories is public ownership and, once you betray that, you betray socialism'. Ben Pimlott, *Harold Wilson*, HarperCollins, London, 1992, p. 218.

25

competition: it changes the relative power of players in the market, changes the boundaries of competition and changes the rules.

The new interdependence

Free market theory assumes that any policy shift along a spectrum stretching from command planning to *laissez-faire* promotes efficiency and prosperity. However, as Amitai Etzioni points out, 'when an economy moves *towards* perfect competition, as the result of deregulating one industry, one *cannot* assume that one will gain some of the benefits of perfect competition';[16] when some of the assumptions of the perfect case are not met, the others are not necessarily desirable. So-called 'second best' economic solutions—departures from the perfect model—are not simply diluted versions of the perfect system: they have their own logic and equilibrium. A host of political, cultural and institutional factors—the welfare state, collective bargaining, and modern corporations for example—create and 'filter' market forces. These filters are not simply exogenous variables bolted on to more or less competitive markets, but central to the logic and incentives of market-based decision-making.

This is fundamental to the debate that has taken place during the last 15 years about the relationship between the market and the state, which has been almost exclusively conducted on the terrain of whether we should have more or less market competition, or more or less state intervention. The key issue has been seen as the 'boundary' of market and state, and the correlating boundaries of private and public choice, and individual and collective decision-making. The case being made here is that to debate the balance between market and state is to misconstrue the issue; the real question is what sort of markets we want to create and what sort of state we want to develop, not how much we have of each. The false polarity of state versus market fails to capture the essential differences that exist between economies in the advanced capitalist world, or the essential choices we face in reforming these societies.

In today's new mixed economy, it is different 'policy regimes' that regulate the relationship between state, market, and citizen. The principles, scope, financing, and mechanisms of state intervention, rather than the number of public companies or the share of government expenditure in GDP, are the key variables for the promotion of opportunity and citizenship. The important point is that there are different sorts of market economy, not simply more or less marketised ones. This is the breakthrough of Michel Albert, whose two models of capitalism, 'Rhenish' and 'neo-American', are derived from a number of qualitative indicators: the structure of the stock market, the organisation of firms, the nature and role of the state. One alternative analysis of the paths of post-war economic

[16] Amitai Etzioni, 'Encapsulated Competition' in *A Responsive Society: Collected Essays on Guiding Deliberate Social Change*, Jossey-Bass, San Francisco, 1991, p. 248.

and social development is provided by Gosta Esping-Anderson, who maps out 'three worlds of welfare capitalism'.[17]

First, he notes a cluster of 'liberal' welfare states like the United States, notable for means-tested benefits, private provision of welfare, and dominance of a relatively untrammelled labour market. Secondly, 'conservative/corporatist' countries like Austria and Germany are clustered together because of their common commitment to a guaranteed minimum level of social rights for all citizens, though with negligible redistributive impact, and a relatively traditional attitude towards social issues like women's work outside the home. Finally, traditionally social democratic economies like those in Sweden and Norway are characterised by high universal benefits, full employment and progressive tax systems.

The interaction of state, market and citizen in each of these clusters of countries produces qualitatively different employment structures, investment choices, and social inequalities. The important issue is not the opposition of market and state but the nature of the interdependence between them; on it depends the logic and rationality of different markets and different economies. It is these differences that an attempt to take the politics out of economics—to separate and counterpose market and state—seeks to deny, and it is these differences that pose a central challenge to traditional models of political economy. The importance of the 'socio-institutional' or 'socio-economic' school is that it blends together social and economic analysis in an original way. The capital-labour relation is now refracted through the accumulated filters of 100 years of government intervention, and models of political economy are beginning to recognise it.

The policy framework

At issue in this debate is the construction of a new political economy for an economic age of global competition, revolution in industry, and deep-seated uncertainty and risk. However, there now exists a profound disjunction between the power and potential of traditional policy instruments on the one hand and modern economic and social demands on the other. In the language of Goran Therborn, the emergence of new patterns of cleavage and conflict, replacing the comfortable assumptions of industrial society and industrial class politics, demand a new era of political intervention.[18] For our purposes, four sets of issues are dominant.

Perhaps the most obvious implication of the preceding analysis is that politics must meet and regulate markets where they exist, which now more

[17] Gosta Esping-Andersen, *The Three Worlds of Welfare Capitalism*, Princeton University Press, Princeton, 1990.

[18] Goran Therborn, 'Swedish Social Democracy and the Transition from Industrial to Post-industrial Politics', in Frances Fox Piven, ed., *Labor Parties in Post-Industrial Societies*, Polity, Cambridge, 1991.

27

than ever means internationally as well as locally and nationally. One does not have to believe in the 'death' of the nation-state (and who could in the light of resurgent nationalisms around Europe?) to accept that the nation state is indeed too small for some of the big problems, and too big for the small ones. The research agenda for the re-regulation of international finance and trade is broad, stretching from the dynamics of European monetary integration to the future of the GATT round, and as Perry Anderson has pointed out, there remains a gaping asymmetry between the need for international regulation and the development of political agencies to carry it out.[19]

The ties between citizens of the European Community, never mind a global community, are especially strained in straitened economic times; but it is international, and supranational, coordination and regulation that now sets the framework for national macro-economic management. An avowedly *political* project, superseding the market-led conception of the last forty years, is now needed to take the Community forward. Within nations, too, the notion of 'free' markets—in training, housing, or more topically in Britain coal—is a mirage. The assertion that there can and must be political responsibility for market outcomes is a first step towards the regeneration of the very notions of public interest and public purpose that are the basis of collective action.

Secondly, it is increasingly clear that the long-standing Keynesian emphasis on demand management presents only half the economic story: to leave the supply side to the fallacies of *laissez-faire* is to torpedo hopes of economic change.[20] To combine equity and efficiency, government intervention is desperately needed on the supply side, most obviously in education and training, but also in investment, research and development and technology transfer. The failure of governments to act as the guardians of posterity through long-term investment in the public infra-structure has produced a debilitating cycle of economic insecurity and social polarisation.

The demand for education reform is perhaps the paradigmatic case. It is not just that, despite all the evidence of social and economic benefit, British pre-school provision is approximately half that of our European neigh-bours, or that vocational training remains patchy in quality and quantity. Notwithstanding the virtual abolition of a formal 11-plus in Britain, the very ethos and structure of our system continues to be based on selection rather than participation, and failure rather than achievement. We remain the only country in the industrialised world with a 'school-leaving' exam at

[19] Perry Anderson, 'The Ends of History', in *A Zone of Engagement*, Verso, London, 1992.

[20] See Egon Matzner and Wolfgang Streeck, 'Introduction: Towards a Socio-Economics of Employment in a Post-Keynesian Economy' and Wolfgang Streeck, 'On the Institutional Conditions of Diversified Quality Production' in Matzner and Streeck, eds., *Beyond Keynesianism: The Socio-Economics of Production and Full Employment*, Edward Elgar, Aldershot, 1991.

15/16, consigning two-thirds of students to make do with narrowly defined vocational curricula. At university level, we defend the privileges of a minority of 'full-time' undergraduates at the expense of part-time and further education students. Meanwhile at work, those with the most education get the most training, leaving the 'skills revolution' a threat to, not an opportunity for, the majority of employees. Any new social contract cannot be built solely on the demand side, and supply-side reform is now a basic necessity for economic as well as social progress.[21]

Thirdly, there is a profound need for a reorientation of economic thinking and strategy to meet the ecological imperative. This cannot mean banning markets; it does mean the collective integration of environmental targets at the heart of government and corporate decision-making. A green economy requires the establishment of environmental incentives at every stage of production. Green taxes offer one short-term mechanism that begins to tackle budgetary and ecological dilemmas.

One paradox of our current situation, brought out by the environmental example, is the parallel development of increased personal freedom on the one hand and social interdependence on the other. On the threshold of the twenty-first century, collective decision-making—at home, at work, and in society—is more important than ever, both to enhance individual autonomy and to further the social interest. Whether making communities safe, developing new products, or protecting the environment, what we agree together, to extend opportunity, promote team-working, or regulate environmental pollution, is the basis for what we do alone.

One example concerns the 'silent' social revolutions underway in advanced industrial societies, and their implications for the balance between work and family life. The potential for personal financial independence for women has clearly been transformed by shifts in social mores and economic demand. But because market relations are also power relations, it will take collective intervention to spread the resources, skills and information essential to personal autonomy. One key example concerns working time, and the triple demand for more jobs to reduce unemployment, shorter working hours to balance work and family life, and greater security of living standards in an era of economic dislocation. Legislation to promote part-time and term-time working (as well as Sunday working), with concomitant changes to benefit regulations, would expand opportunities and financial independence, especially for women. Most important, our notion of full employment, or more weakly 'fuller employment', on which full citizenship to a large extent depends, must be based on a transformation in attitudes about what constitutes a 'real job'.[22]

---

[21] These issues have been an ongoing concern of successive IPPR reports. See for example David Finegold et al., A British 'Baccalauréat': Ending the Division between Education and Training, London, 1990 and David Finegold et al., Higher Education: Expansion and Reform, London, 1992.

[22] See Patricia Hewitt, About Time: The revolution in work and family life, Rivers Oram Press, London, 1993.

Reforms in these areas demand renewed vigour in the search for flexible as well as equitable mechanisms of public administration. In the language of Osborne and Gaebler, the essential precondition for successful state intervention, shaping the grain of market forces in a reflexive civil society, is that government should be concerned above all to 'steer, rather than row', to focus on ends rather than means, long term strategy rather than short term tactics, and organisation rather than provision.[23] This is a useful complement to Pfeffer and Coote's attempt to bring together notions of fitness for purpose, responsiveness and empowerment in their 'democratic' approach to public service delivery which emphasises that 'customers' are also citizens and often joint producers of public services.[24]

Merely to discuss these aspirations for an enabling state suggests that any new synthesis of decentralised decision-making and collective regulation to fill the ideological vacuum must be based on the modernisation of the British state itself. Secrecy, centralisation and exclusivity must give way to a more pluralistic regime of public power. One example concerns the overwhelming evidence from the Continent that local and regional government play a key role in the infrastructure of economic development: in Britain, we need to build a pluralistic regime of public power.

Conclusion

Fifty years ago, Karl Polanyi developed his theses about the politics of market-led growth. He posited the parallel expansion of political regulation and market force—what Goran Therborn calls a 'double historical process'—as the only basis for economic stability. But in the last 15 years, the limitations of Fabian paternalism and Morrisonian nationalisation have been used to discredit all forms of state intervention, as well as the very notion that good government means something more than less government.

It is testimony to the resilience of the 1945 settlement that the Conservatives still consider it necessary to spend five more years taking it apart. But the Left cannot define its project by the defence of what already exists. Required now is a model of political economy adequate to the new interdependence of economic choices and social change. Now is not the time for a return to the *status quo ante*; a second and different counter-revolution is waiting to be made.

[23] David Osborne and Ted Gaebler, *Reinventing Government*, Basic Books, New York, 1992.
[24] Naomi Pfeffer and Anna Coote, *Is Quality Good for You?*, IPPR, London, 1991.

RETICULATED ORGANISATIONS: THE BIRTH AND DEATH OF THE MIXED ECONOMY

GEOFF MULGAN*

DURING the 1980s government enterprises worth an estimated $185bn were sold to the private sector worldwide in much the fastest redrawing of the boundaries of state and market that the world has ever seen. Yet although some of the ideological and fiscal causes of that shift are not in dispute, political and economic commentators have still not satisfactorily explained either why governments of all persuasions across the world came to take over such large swathes of industry in the first place, or why they then came to dispose of them. In what follows I offer one, admittedly partial, explanation by focusing on the shifting relative competences of states and markets in the network or 'reticulated industries' that have always made up the heart of the mixed economy.

The ubiquity of the mixed economy

By the 1980s the typical industrialised country had roughly 10 per cent of GDP in state enterprises, and between 6–8 per cent of all employment (the one significant exception was the USA with only 2 per cent of employment). The UK was typical in that public enterprises accounted for 10 per cent of GDP and 16 per cent of gross fixed capital formation. It was also typical in that the boundaries of this sector had continually fluctuated: in 1919, for example, nationalisation even extended to the pubs of Carlisle to stop them overselling beer.

Between the mid-19th century and the middle of this century huge sectors of industry were taken into public control across the world under models varying from those of Taiwan (where Sun Yat Sen's ideas on the role of public ownership were highly influential),[1] through those of Nehru and Nkruhmah, to those of the post-war reconstruction in countries like France and Britain. State involvement ranged along a continuum from

* Geoff Mulgan is Director of Demos. He was previously policy adviser to Gordon Brown MP. He is the author of *Communication and Control: networks and the new economies of communication*, Polity, London, 1991.

[1] See, for example, Robert Wade's account in *Governing the Market: economic theory and the role of government in East Asian industralisation*, Princeton University Press, Princeton, 1990.

31

direct integration in civil services (like the Post Office until 1969), through arms' length ownership to strategic oversight. Different parts of the state could be dominant: in Britain (with the exception of London) gas, electricity and water were run by municipal authorities until nationalised after World War Two. The Manchester Ship Canal of 1891 was set up jointly by municipal corporations and private stockholders, while bodies like the Metropolitan Water Board were run by boards representing both local authorities and users. In France there was the peculiar evolution of the 'economic mixte' with considerable power held at regional and local level, even after the waves of nationalisation in the 1940s. In the USA many of the utilities were organised, and came to be regulated, at state level. In countries like Italy considerable power was exercised through state holding companies. Despite these differences, however, what is remarkable by historical standards is how similar the various mixed economies were from Chile to Finland, covering a similar set of network and strategies industries, and how dissimilar they were from earlier models such as the state-owned papyrus makers of Ancient Egypt or Colbert's manufactures in 18th century France.

Even as it spread under governments of all political colours, however, the mixed economy always remained the subject of fierce political debate. For 50 years until the 1980s its focus was the precise location of the boundary between public and private. The debate never reached any firm conclusions because, as we shall see, there were no firm theoretical grounds for defining the boundary. Instead, as a broad generalisation, attitudes followed from ideological positions. Labour movements tended to see the publicly-owned part of the economy as prefigurative[2]—a demonstrator of the virtues of public ownership and planning which should be progressively extended (with intervention in private industry by contrast often viewed as an illegitimate subsidy for capital).[3] Nationalist parties tended to view public ownership as the concomitant of nation building, a focus for national economic energy, a counterweight to multi-nationals, and a necessary lever for an effective state, and were therefore content to rest with the commanding heights of the economy. Conservative and liberal parties tended to see public ownership more as a necessary evil where natural monopolies existed, where the essential nature of goods (such as water) precluded the instabilities of market provision, or where private industry failed to respond to fiscal and monetary incentives: at the limit they believed that the state should only run what the markets refused to run.[4] Harold Macmillan, for example, felt

[2] Although there were other traditions. See, for example, G. D. H. Cole, *Economic Tracts for the Times*, 1932, Chapter 12.

[3] Jim Tomlinson, *The Unequal Struggle: British socialism and the capitalist enterprise*, Methuen, London, 1982.

[4] A strong line of liberal argument denied the importance of the difference between public and private ownership. Liberal Party, *Britain's Industrial Future*, 1928; J. M. Keynes, 'The Means to Prosperity' in *Essays in Persuasion*, 1933.

quite at ease in writing in the 1930s that the 'socialist remedy ... should be accepted ... where it is obvious that private enterprise has exhausted its social usefulness'.[5]

One of the striking features of these positions is the extent to which they were political rather than economic in inspiration. The economic theories of public goods and imperfect competition, and the huge Soviet planning literature, only took form in the 1920s and 1930s well after many industries had come into public ownership. The Marxist tradition was famously silent on how public enterprises should be run, and the first formal definition of what a public corporation should be in Britain came from the Crawford Committee on the BBC, hardly an obvious model for industrial organisation (even if Hugh Dalton was later to claim it as such) and yet typical in that its charter set out the Corporation's purpose around extremely vague notions of national interest. In the absence of a clear theory, the public enterprises tended to accumulate their logic from practice. Raymond Williams' comment about broadcasting, that 'the institutions and social policies which get established in a formative, innovative stage—often *ad hoc* and piecemeal in a confused and seemingly marginal area—have extraordinary persistence into late periods, if only because they accumulate techniques, experience, capital and what come to seem prescriptive rights ...', could be applied right across the public sector.

The reticulated state

Although public ownership covered a wide range of industries, some taken over for strategic reasons and some to assist with decline, I want to focus on what has always been the core of the public sector: the 'reticulated' or network industries. These are industries which branch down into everyday life, often with direct physical links to every home or business (as with gas, electricity, telephones or water), or direct delivery (as with the postal service). They are particularly significant for four reasons: they were the first nationalised industries, the first regulated industries, the pioneers of many of the forms of modern business organisation and the first industries to generate a debate about privatisation and deregulation.

Their original significance derived from their role in shaping the boundaries of states' military power. But in the modern period the involvement of states deepened for economic reasons. In Germany, half of all investment in railways up to 1850 came from government, well before Bismarck's nationalisation. In France, where the majority of investment in canals and railways was public, it was 'thanks to the support given by the state that this sector was spared from the bankruptcies and almost spared from the technical failures which it frequently experienced abroad ...'.[6]

---

[5] Harold Macmillan, *The Middle Way*, Macmillan, London, 1938, p. 239.
[6] Quoted in *Cambridge Economic History* VII, p. 249.

33

Even in the USA the telegraph industry was launched with a $30,000 grant from Congress.[7] State support often turned into ownership. In France and Germany railways and telegraph were easily integrated into the state after a period of private ownership (according to Werner Sombart, in Germany the postal services and railways were 'only the civil sections of the army', with generals often acting as senior managers). In Britain the Post Office was run by government, prior to the nationalisation of first the telegraph, then of the telephones and, half a century later, of the railways. In Japan the majority of railways and telecommunications were state owned until the 1980s.

Where ownership remained in private hands, governments had to devise novel methods of regulation. These methods, including many still used in the USA and elsewhere, can be traced to Britain's 1844 'Regulation of Railways Act' which established powers to cap private companies' rates and to impose social obligations. These were justified at the time by William Gladstone in a sophisticated argument which explained why the character of the railway market would preclude competition. Nominally regulations were concerned with only a few parameters, such as price and profit. Over time, however, under the influence of regulations which set standards and rules, the various private network operators came to take on much of the character of civil services. AT&T in the USA was probably the classic case, and as near to a civil service with traded shares as the world has ever seen.

It was these companies which pioneered many of the forms of industrial organisation later adopted in private industry.[8] They had to innovate because when they were first created in the 1830s and 1840s, in the parallel spread of railways and telegraph, and later in the spread of electricity, gas and water distribution, they had no precedents in the private sector. Their sheer scale, both in terms of capital and labour employed and their geographical spread, was of a new order. By the end of the 19th century, they were amongst the largest institutions of their time, with a scale and reach exceeding that of many national governments. They were in all cases pioneers of the 'visible hands' of active planning, forecasting and coordination which came to replace the invisible hand of the market. In France, for example, by the 1880s gas and electricity were the second and third largest companies. In the US Western Union and later AT&T were the largest companies of their times, massive by contrast with the firms of even a few decades before. In Britain, too, according to Chandler, the 'British railroad companies were by far the largest business enterprises . . . during the 19th century . . .'.[9]

In retrospect it is clear that these firms were in many respects more like police forces (which date from the same period) and civil services than

[7] Richard B. Du Boff, 'The rise of communications regulation: the telegraph industry 1844–80', *Journal of Communication*, Summer 1984.

[8] Alfred Chandler, *The Visible Hand*, Harvard/Belknap, Cambridge MA, 1977.

[9] Alfred Chandler, *Scale and Scope*, Belknap, London, 1990, p. 253.

34

other private companies which only later took on this reticulated character with national banking branch networks, cinema chains and franchised fast food stores. Indeed, such national private sector companies were simply not conceivable until national reticulated infrastructures had been built, whether by private or public companies, to distribute goods and to communicate.

As the leading organisations of their time, in terms of scale and scope, their degree of rationalisation, to their immersion in the scientific principles of their engineering communities, it seemed self-evident and most of the world that the network industries should come under the umbrella of modernising government, whether national or local. Governments' techniques of organisation, often developed in colonial administration and the military, were at least on a par with the most advanced forms of private organisation, particularly as mass wars like World War One sharply increased governments' organisational capacities. The military after all had pioneered most of the forms of modern industry: the detailed separation and specification of functions; standardisation and logistical organisation of large quantities over space and time. Mass production, interchangeable parts and complex divisions of labour were familiar in military industries long before they took root more widely. At a local level, too, municipal authorities enjoyed advantages of organisation over their private counterparts. In water, for example, by the second half of the century relative to private firms municipal authorities enjoyed far better access to information and capital.[10]

In short, when the new networks were formed it was natural that they should be close to government and informed by governmental rationalities. It was also the case that the special economic and technological characters of the network industries made them particularly obvious candidates for rationalisation and development by states. The fragmented nature of some of the industries, in stark contrast to others, was an obvious barrier to modernisation: in Britain, for example, electricity was constrained by incompatibilities, gas by the failure of the many local companies to collaborate on research and development. When industries were returned to the private sector, as the railways and coal were after World War One, the effect was usually to delay necessary restructuring and investment. In the absence of effective agencies for restructuring in the private sector, government's role was almost self-evident. In Britain, for example, the Labour nationalisation programme of 1945–51 was largely based on reports from committees of inquiry set up by previous governments: Reid on coal, Heyworth on gas and MacGowan on electricity. The same pattern of apparently non-partisan policy can be found throughout the century. Nationalisation of the Forestry Commission took place under Lloyd George in 1919, while other nationalisations—of the BBC in 1926,

---

[10] J. Hassan, 'The Growth and Impact of the British Water Industry', *Economic History Review*, Vol. 38, 1985, p. 546.

35

the Central Electricity Board in 1927, the London Passenger Transport Board in 1933, the air services under BOAC in 1939, Rolls Royce and what came to be British Leyland in the 1970s—all took place under the Conservatives.

But there was also a more fundamental reason why the state seemed a natural owner. The network industries were designed to provide on a mass scale highly standardised products and services. Their tasks were very similar to the roles being taken on by governments as they developed their nature as services in employment, health and education. Their employment of huge workforces to provide services paralleled precisely the burgeoning bureaucracies of education and welfare. Often the languages began to overlap, as investments in rural railways or telephone lines, and the cross-subsidies between high and low usage parts of the networks, were justified socially. The result was that organisational logics which had been developed by states were readily transferred into the reticulated public organisations, exemplified most clearly perhaps in the way that the nascent telephone industry was explicitly organised around principles derived from the Royal Signals Corps.

Public ownership of these first great network industries established much of the later rationale for public ownership. For Bernard Shaw, for example, 'the extraordinary success of the Post Office, which according to the Manchester School should have been a mess of incompetence and jobbery, had . . . shown the perfect efficiency of state enterprise . . . and the enormous convenience and cheapness of socialistic charges . . .'.[11] The rationale was, in other words, largely economic, or rather techno-economic, in that the economic characteristics flowed from the nature of network technologies. All of the networks shared economic tendencies: high fixed and relatively low marginal costs; long investment lead times; dependence on various types of right of way. These tended to render competition deeply unstable, since owners of competing electricity, telegraph or railway networks would drive prices down to marginal costs until one or other succumbed and a monopoly or cartel could be formed (as was the case in the US railways in the 1870s and the German railways in 1846). As a result investment was irregular and uncertain, bankruptcies common and services unreliable. To the then burgeoning engineering community which did so much to influence the prevailing climate of opinion it was evident that a more rational model of organisation was needed, to be achieved either through municipal or national ownership, or through the kind of regulated monopoly that AT&T engineered in the early years of this century.

[11] G. B. Shaw, 'Transition' in *Fabian Essays in Socialism*, 1889, p. 185.

The argument of monopoly

In a regularly quoted sentence from the 'Wealth of Nations', Adam Smith describes the benefits of public subsidy for canals and roads, the networks of his time. What is less often noticed is that there has never been a fully-fledged economic theory for these sectors: in most of Smith's successors one can find only a few sentences on those sectors which do not fit the standard model. Instead the available theories have always been add-ons; cobbled together from theories of externality and public good, inter-dependent demand and clubs. Even these have only appeared in this century, well after the organising principles and indeed many of the regulatory principles were in place. Even now the emerging network economics rests ill-at-ease in a discipline based on methodological individualism. This contrasts sharply with the theories of planning which, for all their subsequent failings, accumulated a breadth and depth and an obvious practical base in the experience first of war and second of the planned economies.

Despite these theoretical gaps, however, there has, at least since the 1930s, been a reasonably coherent case for public ownership of network industries, drawing loosely on the work of Alfred Marshall and more directly on A. C. Pigou's analysis of private and public goods and the emerging theories of imperfect competition and monopoly. Three sets of arguments stand out, and continue to be involved to this day:

(i) networks are natural monopolies; the optimal size of firms is large, and there are substantial economies of scale (often more precisely economies of density or penetration). Competition can promote an inefficient multiplication of standards. (In Australia, for example, railway gauges were not standardised until the 1950s.)

(ii) networks are producers of quasi-public goods. In other words, they have important spin-off effects not directly captured by their immediate consumers: dynamic effects on economic growth and on social well-being. Some of the goods are also 'club' goods, where benefits grow according to the number of consumers (both directly as with telephones or fax machines, and indirectly by benefits of standardisation and scale).

(iii) networks supply essential goods on which the whole of economic and social life is dependent. Any disruption to supply would threaten the whole economy; public ownership is justified as a precondition for econ-omic security (a justification which could be extended to non-network industries such as steel or coal).

Each of these arguments makes the claim that network industries are concerned with distinct types of value, more social and public, and more defined by interconnection than those of other industries. In precisely the same way, arguments for public ownership of other types of industries have also been based on ideas about value. For strategic industries, for example, proponents of public ownership have pointed to the cumulative

37

nature of the values they produce, their increasing returns to scale and dynamic comparative advantages, which render the market's valuation of an industry and its returns inadequate. More recently, proponents of defensive types of ownership, in steel and ships in the 1960s and 1970s, have typically used arguments posed in terms of a social value, such as the cost of sustaining high unemployment in a region, which overrides the narrow economic values of commercial decisions.

What is significant about these arguments is that they assume that there is little need to worry about institutional forms. Since private monopoly tends towards exploitation of the consumer, it is assumed that public monopoly must be a better alternative. To take just one early example, W. Clarke in the Fabian essays of 1889 is typical in that he deduces, from an analysis of the new trend of concentration and monopoly in both the network industries and in steel and shipping, the self-evident need for state ownership. The question of the state's competence, or lack of it, rarely arose; and although commentators like Tawney recognised that 'when the question of ownership has been settled the question of administration remains for solution',[12] this was generally seen as a technical issue and hardly likely to be beset by fundamental contradictions.

The fallacy of ownership

The case of public ownership was based on an assumption that the legal status of ownership is the central determinant of how property is used and organised. Only an owner can direct, set targets and gather information, safe in the knowledge that there will be no conflict of interest with other stakeholders. Change can be instigated directly, rather than through the thick veil that impedes the use of incentives and directions.

Yet the history of public ownership has been a history of problematic control, of formal power combined with practical impotence: narrowly over such issues as how to set operational guidelines, for example over pricing or required rates of return for investments; more broadly because any enterprise locked into a political system is therefore tied to a shifting and not always compatible collection of goals, which may range from price control and employment creation to regional investment.

Such tensions between control and ownership are not unknown in the private sector. Ironically even at the high point of state ownership the literature on management control and the weakness of ownership, from Berle and Means and many others, was already large. For governments, however, the problems are even more severe. Six sets of problems have characterised public ownership of enterprises:

First, there is an endemic problem of discipline. The discipline of bankruptcy is lost and capital cannot be written off. The disciplines on

---

[12] R.H. Tawney, *The Acquisitive Society*, G. Bell & Sons, London, 1921, p. 149.

labour are weak because of labour's political power. Even the most elementary right of ownership, alienability, is severely constrained.

Second, the absence of mediation and the dispersal of responsibility that occurs in a 'normal' economy has always caused political problems. Unlike private owners governments have no alibis for performance: they cannot blame an impersonal market when jobs are cut and services are closed down.

Third, there is a problem of industrial structure. Many third world countries discovered that nationalisation gave no control over the key points of economic power, the places where commodity prices were determined. Much the same pressures have constrained state-owned British car firms and French computer manufacturers, which found that they could not operate under the conditions of sovereignty that other arms of the state assume.

Fourth, economic globalisation has caused problems. Increasingly state-owned firms found themselves forced to compete in globalised markets that both reduced the salience of the strategic use of a dominant firm, and weakened the ability of national firms to compete overseas because of the constraints of political control. State ownership seriously compromised the independence of companies like British Telecom or Cable and Wireless in bidding for contracts and competing for markets.

Fifth, there has been a consistent problem of motivation. Little systematic attention was ever given to how managers and employers in public enterprises should be motivated. A vague assumption that the public good would engender a more responsible and committed workforce came to mean little. This was less the case where the culture of work was shaped by some overriding ethos—such as the engineering ethos which was so powerful in many of the network industries, or where face to face contact with users gave some meaning to public purpose. Otherwise the public interest turned out to be too diffuse an ideal to motivate.

Sixth, and perhaps most fundamental of all, governments have lacked sufficient organisational and informational capacity fully to govern a large number of enterprises effectively. There is a long history of the successive attempts made in all countries to impose standard accounting and planning procedures in order to mimic some of the workings of a private capital market. The still-unresolved debate about appropriate pricing mechanisms can be dated back to the Ecole des Ponts et Chaussées in France in the early 19th century. Since the early 1960s British governments have sought a 'rationalisation of control and performance by economic criteria ...'.[13] Successive White Papers in 1961 and 1967 sought to tighten decision-making criteria, with 'return on capital' and 'marginal cost pricing' rules, where at the time of nationalisation there had been little more than the requirement that revenues should be sufficient to cover costs. But all the reforms did little to alter the fundamental structural

[13] L. Tivey, ed., *The nationalised industries since 1960*, Allen and Unwin, London, 1973.

problems of ownership. In France the 1967 Nova report made a similar attempt to modernise financial reporting and management. Arrays of monitoring systems were introduced, some dependent on external sources, others on internally generated targets, but all beset by a massive and irresolvable informational asymmetry between the controller and the object of control.

The problem of control

Most of these problems can be subsumed under the more general problem of control: governments in the 20th century can be said to have been engaged in a series of complex experiments into the extent and possibility of control in both society and economy, as they have sought to find out whether the monopoly of power and sovereignty which parliaments and ministries appear to have can be translated into useful control. Enterprises operating in markets represent just one field in which the limitations of control have become apparent, as attention has turned away from the arguments for state ownership and towards the practical competences of governments; the problems of information gathering; of where to locate strategic thinking and intelligence; of how to avoid overload; and more general problems of control common to large bureaucratic organisations whether in private or public sectors.

One effect has been a surprising convergence of developments in both private and public sectors. For state bureaucracies the same logic which at one time fostered empire building has instead led to support for privatisation as a means of retaining power while devolving responsibility. For civil services it may become more attractive to retain overall strategic oversight and some regulatory powers, while operational responsibility is passed down. For private companies, for similar reasons, direct ownership over all aspects of production has been gradually displaced by the techniques of franchising, sub-contracting and licensing, all of which accentuate the market power of the dominant company by allowing it to free itself from the constraints of ownership.

Theoretical erosion

While practical problems chipped away at the confidence of state enterprises their theoretical supports were also proving vulnerable. Significantly it was in the network industries that the erosion of the case was most pronounced and where the most intellectual work was done on alternatives to state ownership and monopoly. The process began in telecommunications as a series of regulatory judgments and economic articles in the USA gradually undermined the claim that telecommunications was a natural monopoly. The networks' monopolies were challenged from the outside inwards as power generation, water purification, gas production, telecommunications equipment, value-added services and premium postal services, all came to be seen as potentially competitive within a relatively normal marketplace.

As this happened, a crucial change took place in the ways in which the values produced by networks were conceived. Where originally these had been understood as producers of standardised services, ones indeed whose very virtue was their simplicity in standardising voltages, band-widths and plugs, by the 1960s this was ceasing to be an accurate descrip-tion. Telecommunications could provide a range of differentiated and customised services, value-added services, mobile services, subscription services. In energy, post and railways too, more specialised needs and models of production were appearing, ranging from small-scale renew-able energy to commuter trains built to function like offices.

Whereas in an earlier period the necessary concentration, rationalisa-tion and standardisation of network industries had been in tune with what governments had become used to in their own work, by the 1970s this was no longer true. The necessary restructuring appeared to go against the grain of normal governance, towards flexibility and devolution, variety and entrepreneurialism, and towards much closer links with users in the definition of services. At the same time competition in international markets required sharp cutbacks in labour and joint ventures with overseas companies.

The historic shift towards more flexible, user-oriented forms of organisation of network industries, seemed impossible to achieve within the institutions and cultures that had been bequeathed. The civil service cultures of provision according to bureaucratically determined and stable levels of service had to be replaced by a more customer-oriented approach. In a sense the solution was obvious: since the competences of states were no longer suitable for the problem at hand, the problems were passed out to institutions which had the competence to run advanced reticulated forms of organisation.

Since the earlier takeover of these core reticulated industries the private sector had, as it were, leapfrogged the public. Its models of reticulated organisation had become far more sophisticated, involving devolution of responsibility to operating units, flexibility in production, the involvement of users in the definition of services, and novel combinations of strict financial oversight and operational decentralisation. Considerable expertise had been built up with techniques of franchising (a model which can be said to have been invented by the Post Office through its thousands of sub post offices), and the provision of guaranteed levels of service and maintenance. The larger transnational private companies also had the advantage of acting as channels for organisational learning from the world's more dynamic economies. The time was therefore ripe for the superior organisational techniques of the private sector to flow back into the public sector, assisted by neo-liberal ideas which helped to bring what

41

Foucault called 'governmental rationality', the conventional thinking about what administrations can achieve, back into line with government's true organisational competences.

These various organisational and theoretical factors behind privatisation can, of course, be exaggerated. Fiscal necessity was usually a more immediate cause, overriding fears about what markets might do to familiar old institutions. In Britain it was the need to raise money for the Exchequer, and to allow companies to raise capital off the PSBR, which was critical in encouraging privatisation of the great network industries. But this was just one factor which converged with many others into a sea-change in attitudes and practices that cut across the political spectrum. In the USA, for example, the deregulationists who did so much to challenge traditional arguments about networks' natural monopolies began on the left, arguing the consumer case for greater competition against the mono-lithic bureaucracies of AT&T and other utilities. In many countries privatisation was supported by trade unions, as in Japan where NTT employees welcomed the prospect of private sector pay. Elsewhere, too, privatisation rarely fits into a simple political model of left and right: in India, for example, it has been a means of displacing the Congress Party; in Eastern Europe a mechanism in some cases for old elites to reestablish their power, in others to displace them; in South Africa, along with competitive tendering, a potential means of displacing the white elite.

New models: beyond the mixed economy

The analysis so far suggests that between the 1960s and 1980s the connec-tions between the prevailing approaches to organisation, and the types of value which they were designed to control, began to break down. What had been governed industries could no longer be easily governed. Their means and ends were no longer self-evident. The result was the theoretical articulation and practical implementation of two different models for resolving the crisis.

The privatised economy

The first option has been to eliminate the distinction between the types of value associated with network industries and those of normal markets, and to remove the state from any but the most minimal involvement. The goal is a wholly privately owned economy, based predominantly on competitive industries and, where this is not possible (with a very strong presumption that competition can be created in most erstwhile 'natural monopolies'), simple regulation that mimics competitive markets. The light tough regulation of the Retail Price Index formulae, which provide a simple rule for utility prices, is an example. Government's role in economic life is confined to elementary regulation, the preservation of

© The Political Quarterly Publishing Co. Ltd. 1993.

stable money and the rule of law. In this model the disciplines provided by shareholders on the one hand, and consumers in a competitive market on the other, are taken to be sufficient policers of efficiency. The idea that the state can in any way substitute in determining public interest ends for consumers is rejected.

The regulated economy

The second option can be called the 'regulated economy'. The idea that network industries involve distinct types of value is retained, but matched with a new machinery for control which separates ownership from control, regulation from operation. The ownership structure of the privatised economy is combined with a highly active regulatory state, acting through agencies at arms' length from government itself with wide powers to influence decision-making. Utilities are controlled through formulae such as the RPI+x rules, but also through linking in other goals such as household penetration in the case of telecommunications, quality of service (for example in water), social provision and regional spread. Regulators can also be given broader strategic powers to ensure the development of new technologies or industrial capacity. In short, a series of public interests are defined by the state and policed by agencies in what is no longer a mixed economy, but rather a combination of private owner-ship and public control in which regulations, preferably transparent, define the public interest.

Regulated competition

Neither of these models is yet in place in a pure form, although there is a clear momentum towards them as two poles of a continuum of 'regulated competition'. Both, however, have fundamental flaws. The privatised economy model remains acutely vulnerable to the criticism that it will underprovide public goods and goods with externality effects; even if these can be reflected in taxes or subsidies, government's greater distance from the practical knowledge of these industries will tend to make any such interventions less effective. With environmental issues rapidly enter-ing the world of the utilities through the energy issues of generation and conservation, through the problems of water quality and through the impacts of transport and communications networks on energy usage, this model seems unlikly to prove sustainable. In other respects, too, the attempted depoliticisation of the networks implied by full privatisation is already running into obstacles, since although many of the types of value being produced by networks are becoming more differentiated, basic services retain overwhelming preponderance, and are treated by users as different in nature from other services. Another barrier to depoliticisation is that far from passing decision-making out of government, one effect of privatisation has been to create a new and powerful lobby on government:

43

© The Political Quarterly Publishing Co. Ltd. 1993.

what could be called a 'privatisation complex', a market distortion of government, based on private contractors and other providers dependent on public money.[14]

The fundamental flaws of the regulatory model by contrast are primarily informational. Just as finance ministries could rarely know much about the strategic choices or underlying costs of complex networks, so has it proved immensely hard for regulators to get a grip on the complex facts of regulated companies. Such asymmetries may be unavoidable, particularly when in a competitive market companies have stronger arguments for non-disclosure. But even if full information were to be available, it remains hard to see how regulatory agencies could arrive at adequate and transparent definitions of the public interest when, despite more than a century as a fully-fledged discipline, economics can offer no usable concepts of public good or externality.

The problems inherent to these two 'ideal-type' options therefore seem likely to push policy makers in new directions. One set of options would bring a return to greater state involvement, but now in new forms:

(i) the first would involve a move towards what could be called the 'directive state'. Instead of operating either through ownership or through arms' length agencies, government would define and police overall strategies for the network industries. The traditional strategic role of government would be revived, but in the modern form of the executive agency, able to evolve its own culture and techniques, and empowered to control access to markets in order to impose a relatively small number of social environmental and technological requirements.

(ii) The second possible direction of development would be towards a mercantilism of reticulated industries. Their domestic conditions of operation would be determined primarily by their need to compete effectively in other countries. High prices for customers would be justified by the need to generate surplus capital for acquisitions abroad. Private or minority state ownership would be combined with aggressive support by government. Elements of these approaches are already visible in the US government's treatment of AT&T and the regional Bell Operating Companies, in the UK government's treatment of British Telecom and Cable and Wireless, and in arguments surrounding the future organisation of gas and electricity industries in a more openly competitive European marketplace, where innovations such as superconductivity will make it technically easier for energy suppliers to distribute energy across very large areas.

(iii) A third option would be to democratise the concept of the public good. Traditionally public goods, and quasi-public goods have been largely beyond qualification. Externalities, though integrated into cost-benefit analysis techniques, are always in practice experts' estimates. In recent years, however, debates around environmental values have led to

[14] Paul Starr, *The Limits of Privatisation*, Economic Policy Institute, Washington, 1987.

the beginnings of a revolution in the concept as public preferences are sought and turned into quantities. The informational tasks of the market in transmitting private preferences are replicated through collective decision making, partly as a way of ensuring legitimacy for decisions, partly as a way of shifting responsibility out from the core of the state. This may be one long-term effect of innovations such as the citizens charters, which could be turned into tools for making choices about public priorities.

A second set of options by contrast would involve a further diminution of direct state involvement:

(i) one would be a move towards greater self-regulation. Networks would be governed by legally defined obligations and interests, but rather than being subject to enforcement by a single regulatory agency, the policing function would be passed out to a dispersed auditing profession, required to govern itself according to agreed criteria. To a large extent this is already the case with financial reporting; it is currently spreading rapidly to environmental issues, and may evolve further into areas such as ergonomics, training policy and even decision-making practices. The aim would be to overcome some of the informational asymmetries of the agency model by embedding regulation and public interests more deeply within organisations. The weakness is, of course, that such auditing depends on the genuine independence and public motivation of those doing it.

(ii) An alternative solution to the informational overload problem that is endemic to government involvement in the economy would redefine government's role away from the totality of what industries do and towards what could be termed their interfaces, such as the service delivered to the home, the interconnection of networks, the terms of competition and the terms of trade or interconnection at an international level. Only at these points would public interests be defined and given regulatory or legal backing, leaving to organisations themselves the problem of ensuring that requirements are met. In embryo this has been the rationale of the Open Network Architecture and Open Network Provision rules for telecommunications in the USA and Europe respectively.

Conclusions

The mixed economy has often been interpreted as a common sense compromise between the extremes of *laissez-faire* and planning. What I have shown is that in an important set of sectors it arose rather because the new models of organisation that were developing within governments spread into the economy, starting with the great reticulated organisations. These rational, standardising, technology-driven bodies, organised in national hierarchies with local nodes, became obvious candidates for public ownership, because competitive markets without adequate capital were often simply not capable of providing stable levels of service.

Sixty years ago, the two sectors were more obviously in balance, and the Bridgman Committee justified keeping the Post Office within the civil service with the argument that 'overcentralisation, absence of initiative, lack of imagination and failure to give appropriate representation to technical functions are faults which are to be found in the sphere of private as well as government administration ...'. Since then, however, the balance has tilted decisively away from government. The penetration of the economy by government has gone into reverse and the private sector's competences in reticulated organisation have evolved rapidly, providing a practical basis for market ideas to spread beyond more obviously economic functions into government itself, into everything from prisons to schools and hospitals. In all these parts of the state internal markets are coming into use, and ideas such as those popularised by David Osborne and Ted Gaebler[15] for introducing competition, performance measurements and incentives into bureaucracies to make them innovative, responsive and entrepreneurial, are gaining ground. The momentum is such that it is hard to conceive of any early return to widespread public ownership unless the micro-reform of public services somehow enables them to jump ahead of conservative private institutions (like the crudely reticulated high street banks, which leave almost no autonomy to branch managers).

This flood of private sector ideas into government can be interpreted, following Harold Perkin, as a victory of the private sector professionals over the public sector ones. But it may be better understood as a new twist in the long history of what Jacques Donzelot has called the 'hybridisation of the private and the public, the state and the civil', where the big change is that, whereas previously the state handed down answers to society's needs, now across many spheres the problems of the state are being devolved so that society becomes implicated in the task of resolving them.[16] This can be seen most dramatically perhaps in the mass privatisation of the Treuhandanstalt in Germany, of Kraus in Czechoslovakia and the Yeltsin government in Russia, more modestly in the hiving off of public enterprises in the West.

If this analysis is correct, then the swing away from public ownership is not simply an effect either of medium-term political cycles of the kind that Karl Polanyi and Albert Hirschman have analysed, or of that drunkard's walk of progress which leads nations from the failures of market driven systems to public ownership and back again, with some never-quite-attained happy medium in between that is always overshot. Nor can it be analysed with the distinctions drawn by Michel Albert and others to categorise the different types of modern capitalist society. These cannot explain why, for example, both the German and Japanese governments

[15] David Osborne and Ted Gaebler, *Reinventing Government*, Basic Books, New York, 1991.
[16] Jacques Donzelot, 'The mobilisation of society' in G. Burchell *et al.* (ed), *The Foucault Effect*, Harvester, Hemel Hempstead, 1991, p. 178.

have felt the need to privatise their telecommunications operators, and why governments of both left and right have restructured their reticulated industries in similar ways. Instead, the changing balance between public and private, state and market solutions, cannot be separated from the organisational forms and competences which each brings to bear. It is with these, and with public and private organisations' practical ability to recognise and solve problems in everything from energy to prisons and from universities to childcare, that any useful argument now has to begin.

CATHOLICISM, CHRISTIAN DEMOCRATS AND 'REFORMED CAPITALISM'

JONATHAN BOSWELL*

AFTER World War II, a species of 'reformed capitalism' staked out a foothold in large parts of Western Europe. The new mutation brought mildly redistributive, stabilising, humanising modifications. But by the early 1990s a regression, pioneered in the U.S. and the U.K., was becoming widespread. Even the much admired co-operative-corporatist capitalism of central and northern Europe became vulnerable to a deflation-ridden, casino-volatile system in which social division and injustice were increasing.

I believe we can better understand the sources of post-1945 reformed capitalism, even find some pointers towards a desirable replacement, by considering a little-studied interaction between religion and economic forces in modern times.

My first thesis is that, from the 19th century, Catholic social thinking and organisation nurtured a form of communitarianism with the potential to help to modify capitalism; but also, more radically, to go on contesting even its reformed versions. Secondly, I argue that between the 1940s and the 1960s social Catholicism, plus a Christian Democracy largely derived from it, contributed a great deal to reforming capitalism in Western Europe. It added to markets and state control the rudiments of a seriously under-estimated co-operativist third force in political economy, one which included strong elements of interclassism, consociation and mediation. Thirdly, this convergence retreated; capitalism regressed; Christian democratic politics declined. I suggest, though, that a Catholic communitarian critique still offered clues, but alongside other communitarian tendencies, towards a more radical, 'counter-cultural' and probably much longer-term reform.

From its early 19th century beginnings, modern Catholic social thought relied on religious resources (including theology), but drew at least as much on 'natural law' or 'an almost instinctual appreciation of a rule of behaviour appropriate to rational human beings' (a wider philosophical discourse). Both elements flowed through an official stream, particularly after 1891 (mainly comprising papal social teachings), and an experimental stream involving Catholic philosophers, publicists, literary

* Jonathan Boswell lectures at the Von Hügel Institute, St Edmunds' College, Cambridge. He is author of many works, including *Community and the Economy, the Theory of Public Co-operation*, Routledge, London, 1990.

figures and activists, sometimes clerical, usually lay. Recent scholarship tends to confirm the experimental stream's importance *vis-à-vis* the official, whether as precursor, developer or, sometimes, contestant, also the existence of marked, often persistent tensions between the diverse strands of social Catholicism.[1]

All these strands adhered to what Nussbaum nicely terms a 'thick vague theory' of human goods:[2] a normative anthropology, in this case a concept of human persons, each of infinite worth, developing towards fulfilment primarily via relationships involving companionship, mutual help and shared virtue-seeking. Although personalist community as supreme social value was thought to be partly spiritual and so beyond human judgment, certain measurable obstacles to it seemed clear: social atomisation, over-centralisation, an unjust distribution. Clarity as to its concrete approxima-tions emerged more slowly, through concepts of 'free associativeness', 'civic conscience', 'mutual aid', 'co-operative association', 'economic responsibility' etc.[3]

Three corollaries followed. First, personalist community would be pluriform: not an all-enveloping collective, not mere pluralism, nor just minuscule *Gemeinschaft*, but spheres of sociality vital for the good life: familial, territorial, occupational, cultural-religious, universal as well as small. Secondly, it would demand both personal and group freedoms, a wide diffusion of responsibilities: hence the 'subsidiarity' concept, better expressed as power-sharing, or successively larger authorities as sup-porters or supplementers, not displacers, of smaller ones. Thirdly, com-munity could not exist without solidarity towards the poor and a radical upraising of them. Hence an emancipatory, redistributive element, going well beyond traditional charitable works: an attack on social injustices or, in recent jargon, 'a preferential option for the poor', with such notions as 'the primacy of labour over capital' and concerns for factory legislation, free trade unions, a living wage, social security etc.[4]

Catholics often exaggerated the gap between this ideal type pattern and their secular opponents, individualistic liberalism and collectivist social-ism.[5] Condemning those ideologies, they also sought to adapt and absorb large parts of them. Thus, 'equality' was censured in its acquisitive, mechanical, individualistic forms, but then differentially reinstated as the

---

[1] F. P. McHugh, 'Christian social theory', in V. Outhwaite and T. Bottomore, eds., *A Dictionary of 20th-century Social Thought*, Blackwell, Oxford, 1993. P. Misner, *Social Catholicism in Europe*, Darton, Longman and Todd, London, 1991.

[2] M. Nussbaum, 'Aristotelian Social Democracy', in R. B. Douglass, G. Mara and H. Richardson, eds., *Liberalism and the Good*, Routledge, New York and London, 1990.

[3] Leading expositors here included Muller, Buchez, Donoso Cortes, Von Ketteler, Von Vogelsang, La Tour du Pin, Toniolo, Scheler, Pesch, Sturzo, Sangnier, Maritain, Mounier, Lebret, Perroux, Dossetti, Moro.

[4] (1) was there from the first; (3) gathered steam from the 1860s onwards; the libertarian aspects of (2) took longest to develop.

[5] A polar example was E. Keller 1865, 'Either rapacious individualism offset by totalitar-ian régimes, or Catholicism', cited in Misner, *op. cit.*, p. 151.

49

key 'anti-poverty' component of community. 'Democracy', which official Catholicism delayed and dithered about for far too long, was heavily invested with ideas of social responsibilities as well as rights. Such recycling applied still more to 'liberty'. Refused supremacy, denied indefinite expandibility, above all excoriated in its classic individualistic, 'selfish' forms, liberty was yet readmitted within the communitarian frame. Much liberty would be justified, indeed demanded, by true community. But always, the peak concept or maximand was to be, not freedom for its own sake, but personalist community.

Outside the camp, Catholic social thinking was more often discounted than attacked: sometimes seen as reactionary, aprioristic, a tool of ecclesiastical power or a cloak for political opportunism, often as no more than a 'rag bag' or 'hotch potch'. As a 'thick' species of communitarianism, more intense than comparatively 'thin' forms and more conceptually ramified, Catholic social thought stood at a tangent to libertarianism and egalitarianism. It offered a critique, not only of capitalism and collectivism, but also of underlying premises shared by both. Through its history, a familiar tension was constantly repeated between propitiation and prophecy, reformism and radicalism, a mediating, pacifying side and some starker counter-cultural ones.[6]

Interclassism, consociation, economic moderation

At first sight, the thesis of a linkage between this ideology and the historic reforms in capitalism after World War II may seem exiguous. It is not simply that the sweeping concepts and the ethical idealism appear highly abstract, nor just that the personalist-communitarian rhetoric was often deficient in empirical back-up or prescriptive content. There is also an apparent contradiction with a tradition which tended to marginalise economic concepts and problems.

Like romantic social thought generally, social Catholicism detested classical economics. With the neo-classicism of 'rational economic man' and competitive equilibria its mental and moral chasm was no less deep. The glacial distance from mainstream economic theory persisted. It was exceptional for Catholic writers to make even a cursory bow towards markets and competition. Of course, the quarrel with Marxism was no less acute, and eventually a lot more voluminous. There were, it's true, successive importations from economic historians and institutionalists, so called 'social economics' and, by the 1930s, proto-Keynesianism. But the mainstream was un-, a- or even anti-economic. Where economic concepts

---

[6] According to Gramsci, 'a collection of positive and negative polemics ... without constructive value': see T. Godéchot, *Le Parti Démocrate Chrétien Italien*, Paris, 1964, p. 108. For an extreme mix of critiques see G. Poggi in S. Woolf, ed., *The Rebirth of Italy*, London, 1972.

directly entered, as notably with Ryan, Pesch, Perroux, the subordination to politics, social theory and, above all, social ethics, was marked.[7]

A first clue to disentangling the paradox lies in a seemingly abstract carry-over of Catholic thought into political economy, the theory of *interclassismo*. Like much else, this betrayed organic concepts of unity-in-diversity or complementarity derived from Greek thought, even trinitarian doctrine. Basically, ideal type *interclassismo* implied co-operation and consensus between roughly equalised economic interests performing essential and complementary social functions.

According to its chief exponent Luigi Sturzo, priest, sociologist, politician and Christian democrat pioneer from the 1900s to the 1940s, *interclassismo* would encompass workers, peasants, middle classes, entrepreneurs, but with their respective power altered to the advantage of workers and peasants, and with the latter as principal change-agents (though top-down concessions especially by the entrepreneurs could help). Strong trade union and political action, sustained by a culture of self-education and self-discipline animated by Christian principles, would be vital, as would the non-violent, symbolic strike (sponsored in action by Sturzo himself); also universal suffrage on a PR basis and a wide redistribution of private property, especially land, through legislation and taxation.[8]

This elastic ideal offered plenty of material for dispute within the camp. The timid could emphasise its pacifism and respect for middle groups, radicals its rationale for worker struggle and a contestation of arguably parasitic elements like the rentier, the monopolist, the property speculator. Yet the concept brought out a certain contrast between Catholic and *other* conservatives, Catholic and *other* leftists. Even the most moderate socialist aimed ultimately at a displacement so that for him class co-operation could be no more than a reluctant, enforced strategy; whereas even the most radical of Catholic militants would tend to accept class co-operation as a moral goal so that, for him, it was the class struggle, for all its militancy and apparent durability, which would be provisional.[9] This contrast would become clearer in so far as Sturzo's political model eventually emerged: a Catholic, democratic, reformist party which would *itself* incorporate all the main classes and *itself* seek to pilot their co-operation.

A partly-related pursuit, equally exporting Catholic communitarianism into the economic domain, was to criss-cross the market economy with

[7] P. Misner, *op. cit.*, J. P. Ryan, *Distributive Justice*, New York, 1908. R. Mulcahy, *The Solidarist Economics of Heinrich Pesch*, New York, 1952. F. Perroux, *Capitalisme et Communauté de Travail*, Paris, 1938.

[8] G. de Rosa, *L'utopia politica di L. Sturzo*, Brescia, 1972. A. di Giovanni and E. Guccione, *Politica e sociologia in L. Sturzo*, Massimo, Milan, 1981.

[9] P. Misner, *op. cit.*, pp. 258–9. W. L. Patch, *Christian Trade Unions in the Weimar Republic*, Yale University Press, New Haven, Conn., 1985. J. Zirnheld, *Cinquante Années de syndicalisme Chrétien*, Paris, 1937.

51

consociative institutions. If economic life was not to be dominant or autonomous or centralised, if it was to be humanised and to promote the dispossessed, a fabric of interweaving institutions would be needed, a civil society for, in and around the economy. Hence, most obviously, the many projects for enterprise, industry or national guildism, free association, corporatism, co-operativism. If socialists typically dreamt of publicly owned, statist (or sometimes worker-run) bodies, social Catholics repeatedly advocated horizontal, contact-promoting, cross-sectional, inter-group institutions. Here, though, they could be over-hopeful as to the community or relational gains from improved contiguity alone.[10]

Further, if social and ethical pursuits were to prevail, the economy would need not only such criss-crossing, institutionally, but also corralling or encircling. The pursuit of a socio-ethical re-integration of economic life was one factor behind the persistent emphasis on 'intermediate organisations' also in the political sphere, on subsidiarity and revived communes and regions. It found some reflection in a federal or confederal-flavoured Europeanism. As it emerged particularly after 1918, Christian social or Christian democratic Europeanism tended to be socio-political in concept and far from classic free trade, commerce or market-led, even where economic considerations played a part.[11]

A third factor with marked implications eventually for reformed capitalism was the ethos of economic moderation, the perennial desire to restrain acquisitiveness.[12] In some contexts, whatever its benefits for the soul and for *communio*, such restraint could be economically adverse. Yet its economic moment might arrive in a regime of high employment, inflationary fears and excessive consumer and welfare expectations. Not that this consummation would have impressed the early social Catholics even if they could have predicted it. Its economic utility would be a consequence unintended, not even greatly desired. Much the same applies to the theme of mediating and moderating sectional demands, whose role as an aid to steady economic growth was far from central even for the post-1945 social Catholics. As for the conflicts between competition and state control, in contrast with other and, from the first, more economically-minded, ideologies, Catholic communitarianism could even enjoy a paradoxical comparative advantage. Moderation, even uninterest, might offer the chance of economic flexibility without trauma.

Other tendencies arrived at the mixed economy through many decades of painful revisionism. Their panaceas became so skewed by exceptions as eventually to call into question the original utopias, even their underlying

[10] For a careful perspective see R. L. Camp, *The Papal Ideology of Social Reform*, Leiden, 1969.
[11] P. Van Zeeland, *Regards sur l'Europe*, Brussels, 1932. R. Poidevin, *Robert Schuman, homme d'état*, Imprimerie Nationale, Paris, 1986. R. Papini, *L'Internationale démocrate-chrétienne* 1925–1986, Cerf, Paris, 1988. For the 'anti-sovereignty' view underlying all this see J. Maritain, *Man and the State*, Chicago, 1952.
[12] A. Fanfani, *Catholicism, Capitalism and Socialism*, London, 1935.

philosophies. A foretaste was J. S. Mill's liberal competitive paradigm, at once attended by a long, weighty list of statist exceptions.[13] Many devotees of market competition came to climb, though less presciently than Mill, mountain after mountain of contradiction to their original faith. From the left, the same journey was followed in the opposite direction, perhaps more painfully, by social democrats and Marxists. 'Revisionism', or coming to terms with mixed economy, was long delayed, stressful, divisive, and generally unconvincing. By the late 20th century, the left had shifted towards uneasy compromise. A residual *credo* awkwardly cohabited with endless deviation towards its opposite, even partial surrender to a resurgent individualism.

By contrast, social Catholicism merged the initial polarities, if only vaguely and rhetorically, from the start. Indeed, this was partly why it exasperated its rivals. It remained sure that a lot of decentralised initiative was necessary and desirable *and* much intervention; semi-autonomous economic units *and* an active state; private property ownership widely diffused but with its use much circumscribed. This combination applied to all the leading theorists and, in generally more abstract terms, to the papal encyclicals from *Rerum Novarum* 1891 to *Centesimus Annus* 1991. But it would not have been possible without a third factor again reflecting the basic value of community, namely a pursuit of social co-operation. Embryonically, this brought a further paradox. Suppose co-operation were actively pursued within the economy, but not so much for the sake of economic success as for the sake of human relational goods or personalist community. Could greater economic success ensue partly as an oblique spin-off?

This would be difficult to test. For a long time economic co-operativism had to be attempted by the Catholic labour and agricultural organisations in tiny oases and against great odds. Through the 19th century three types of such experiment receded: the Christian workshop or factory as a sub-category of religious community; the 'mixed' association of employers and workers within existing capitalist power structures (premature corporatism); and the workers' association under upper-class leadership (social paternalism). Longer-lived tensions came from issues of church authority or papalist centralism. Major blows were dealt by the partial reaction under Pius X (1903–14), inter-war Fascist adventures in Italy, Austria, Spain, and, from time to time, conservative elements within the Vatican.[14]

By 1914, however, through most of Western Europe, a firm foothold had been won by self-standing agricultural and other co-operatives and Catholic labour movements. By the 1920s, after long struggles, proto-Christian democratic parties, also self-governing, were appearing. This

[13] J. S. Mill, *Principles of Political Economy*, 1848, Book V, ch. XI, reprinted by Penguin Books, Harmondsworth, 1970.

[14] See P. Misner, *op. cit.*; also M. P. Fogarty, *Christian Democracy in Western Europe 1820–1953*, London, 1957.

53

happened meteorically but briefly in Italy, marginally in France, solidly in the Low Countries. But it finally took the aftermath of Fascism, Nazism and World War II to resurrect or expand it.

Competition and direction with co-operation as pivot

In practice, the sort of economy which Christian democratic and social Catholic movements tended to encourage in the years after World War II, though far from their ideal, bore some resemblances to it. The impetus was towards a largely market, private enterprise sub-structure, a *dirigiste* super-structure, but above all, social co-operation as the attempted fly-wheel or pivot.

The parameters were set, of course, by reconstruction, inflation fears, international economic co-operation, the Cold War, pressures for full employment and welfare. In conventional terms, macro-economically, the Christian Democratic parties were left-of-centre, not far from the socialists, in France, Belgium, the Netherlands. In Italy, the hyper-eclectic *Democrazia Cristiana* (DC), stretching from Christian socialists to extreme conservatives, was led from the centre, initially by De Gasperi. The more traditionalist Austrian party was conciliatory towards the socialists. In West Germany, the CDU's right-centredness became entrenched early: a product of Adenauer's sway, conservative, liberal and Protestant influences, and distrust of a post-war S.P.D. intransigently led by Schumacher, already striding the left-centre, and still nationalistic, anti-clerical, secularist and theoretically Marxist-collectivist.[15] But for purposes of my argument, these differences matter little. What counts is the central tendency towards a synthesis of markets and direction, softened, complemented and overarched by co-operative pursuits.

A first test came with the late 1940s reactivation of competitive market forces chiefly in Germany and Italy. Behind this lay arguments about discredited Nazi and Fascist controls, private investment, inflation, Communist obstruction. But could liberal market policies be reconciled with Catholic social ideology? The Catholic left opposed them. The Christian Democrats' post-war manifestos had not predicted them. The leaders who sanctioned them, chiefly De Gasperi and Adenauer, tough, wily and devout men nurtured on Catholic culture and social movements, could have had a hard job on their hands. But Catholic thought was not unhelpful. It made no provision for the issues of investment, trade, currency, output etc. addressed by an Erhard or an Einaudi, thus rendering pragmatism easier. It had never condemned, and nearly always tended to tolerate, moderate degrees of competition. It provided much positive

---

[15] A. J. Heidenheimer, *Adenauer and the C.D.U.*, reprinted Ann Arbor, Michigan, 1977; K. Adenauer, *Memoirs 1945–53*, London, 1965; L. J. Edinger, *Kurt Schumacher*, London, 1965.

support for private property, private initiative, non-centralised decision making. And the assumption seems to have been that large infusions of market forces could be benignly accommodated within the larger, longer-term whole it offered.[16]

This had long embraced diverse strands of *dirigisme*. Past involvements in factory legislation, social security measures and inter-war New Dealism offered many precedents. Christian Democratic statism was to be most explicit in the Low Countries, Austria and France, more covert within the 'social market' rubric of West Germany. But it is a familiar point that even there, despite the rhetoric of 'anti-planning', public intervention was ubiquitous. Everywhere, Christian Democrats accepted or presided over substantial nationalisations, high taxation and public spending, discriminatory fiscal policies, active industrial and agricultural policies. Under their aegis regional policies burgeoned, from Wallonia through Bavaria to the *Mezzogiorno*. Often with West Germany in the van, their social security programmes were comparable in many ways with those of European social democracy.[17]

At first sight, this looks like a simple dualistic balancing act. In contrast with both left and right, for whom reformed capitalism brought much deviation, even ideological *angst*, the Christian Democrats might seem distinctive if only in capaciously welcoming both markets and *dirigisme*. Thus, the alternating coalitions of the French, Dutch and Belgians, now with economic liberals, now with socialists. Thus, the late 1940s turn to markets by Adenauer and De Gasperi. Thus, some later welfare-ist shifts in Germany, and the trend towards centre-left economic thinking in Italy (Saraceno, Taviani, Vanoni, Fanfani) culminating in the centre-left governments of the 1960s. Thus, too, the repeated reliance of Christian Democratic-led governments on departmental carve-ups between their own socio-economic wings. Typically, economics and trade would be allotted to Christian Democratic rightists, social and labour ministries to the (usually trade unionist) Christian Democratic left.[18]

All this could be viewed according to taste as unprincipled, opportunistic, 'anti-ideological' or merely pragmatic. No doubt it was a bit of all of these, but it was also something more. For the dualism only made sense because of a third, more genuinely differentiating factor, the pursuit of co-operation in both the economy and politics.

Here we confront a major gap in conventional political economy,

[16] See particularly P. Scoppola, *La Proposta Politica di De Gasperi*, Il Mulino, Bologna, 1978; also P. Weymar, *Konrad Adenauer*, London, 1957; and K. Adenauer, *Memoirs*, *op. cit.*

[17] G. Hallett, *Social Economy of West Germany*, London, 1973. P. Flora and A. Heidenheimer, eds., *The Development of Welfare States in Europe and America*, New Brunswick and London, 1981.

[18] On the last point see T. Godéchot, *op. cit.*; G. Braunthal, *The Federation of German Industry in Politics*, Ithaca, New York, 1965; F. Spotts, *The Churches and Politics in Germany*, Middleton, Conn., 1973, E. Callot, *L'Action et l'oeuvre politique du Mouvement Républicain Populaire*, M. Rivière, Paris, 1978.

JONATHAN BOSWELL

indeed a systematic philosophical bias, its concentration on markets and direction. Political theory's long obsession with liberty and equality, downgrading a full treatment of community, is carried forward or even compounded by an equally dominant duopoly in economic thinking. This obscures the importance of the third term: what I call 'public co-operation' in the economy. Such a concept is badly needed in order to make sense of a range of significant phenomena too often addressed separately—*Sozial-partnerschaft*, *freiwilligie Disciplin*, 'economic responsibility', 'liberal corporatism'—in which Christian Democracy played a (perhaps the) leading part.[19]

Scholars have discussed Christian Democracy's favouring of joint consultation and *Mitbestimmung*; its subsidiarist regional emphasis; the way in which a 'liberal corporatism' favourable to consensus and anti-inflationary pay policy flourished under its auspices in the Low Countries, Austria, West Germany; and its solid *rapport* with the EEC in the broad sense of that term, pioneered by Schuman, Monnet and Adenauer in coal and steel.[20] Political contributions no less useful to reformed capitalism have also been analysed: the 'centrism' of most of the parties, their focal role in coalitions, particularly under PR, their coalitionist propensities even when endowed with parliamentary majorities, their role as demo-cratic guardians in Italy and Germany.[21] For that matter, some directly related defects or ambivalences are reasonably familiar, notably overlong tenures of power leading eventually to much fatigue and conservative drift, and *clientelismo* or bloated public sectorism, at least in the Italian case.[22]

However, an integrated view of the co-operativist institutions and practices has been lacking, along with a recognition of their linkages with Catholic social thought. I am suggesting that indirectly, unintentionally, this thought provided two further levers towards economic success. Its marginalisation of economics produced a usefully agnostic flexibility towards market-statist policy mixtures. At the same time, the approach tended to make economic co-operation 'work' precisely through the stance towards it which was not primarily economic-instrumentalist but ethical-intrinsicist. Equally lacking, however, has been a more searching look at some of the underlying dynamics, and it is to these that I now turn.

[19] See J. Boswell, *Community and the Economy, the Theory of Public Co-operation*, Routledge, London, 1990.
[20] H. J. Spiro, *The Politics of German Codetermination*, Cambridge, Mass., 1958. R. E. M. Irving, *The Christian Democratic Parties of Western Europe*, Allen and Unwin, London, 1979.
[21] See for example W. T. Bluhm, *Building an Austrian Nation*, New Haven, Conn., 1976; V. Bogdanor and D. Gladdish in V. Bogdanor, ed., *Coalition Government in Western Europe*, Heinemann, London, 1983; and A. Lijphart, *The Politics of Accommodation, Pluralism and Democracy in The Netherlands*, Berkeley, California, 1975.
[22] G. Pasquini in P. Lange and S. Tarrow, eds., *Italy in Transition*, Cass, London, 1980; D. Sassoon, *Contemporary Italy*, Longman, London, 1986; R. Leonardi and D. A. Westman, *Italian Christian Democracy*, Macmillan, Basingstoke and London, 1989.

56

Active cross-sectionalism, allied social movements, Catholic culture

First, active cross-sectionalism. In the six future EEC countries Catholics varied from large minorities to large majorities. Between the 1940s and the 1960s their electoral mobilisation by the Christian Democrats was intense. Religious loyalties and clerical support saw to that, along with anti-Communism and some vigorous leadership. Only in France, its Catholicism long fragmented, did the Christian Democrats fail to scoop up less than a huge majority of the Catholic vote. But the important point is that that electorate tended to be strongly multi-class.[23] If this was hardly original in itself, what followed was more so. For it was on this foundation that the parties, again partly spurred on by Catholic social ideas, erected a first approximation to *interclassismo*: a representation and consociation of the different sectors within party structures, parliament or government.

Such intra-party corporatism (though by now this term was discredited) revived earlier practices from the Low Countries, the *Zentrum* and the *Partito Popolare*. Major imbalances in a social class's representation might be corrected higher up with the implicit aim of a broad parity. The system often favoured the rural and middle classes, while big business short-circuited it through informal access and, sometimes, finance, perhaps particularly in Germany and Italy. If this was a long way from Sturzo's vision, each major socio-economic sector at least had substantial representation. Thus, the Catholic labour organisations formed one of Christian Democracy's four vocational pillars in Belgium and the Netherlands, the peasants and farmers another. In Italy the labour and left-wings together typically held between 25 per cent and 30 per cent of both party congress votes and parliamentary seats.[24]

It appears reasonable to attribute some wider spin-offs to this form of socio-economic federalism: a further impetus towards the 'export' of corporatism in so far as the home-grown product proved habit-forming; a formation of political leaders from most social or economic classes; their pre-exposure to a wide range of interests; some better informed policy making; and, as Lijphart suggests, mediation between all these groups as a help towards mediation in government. In addition, business-labour conflicts might be softened by the interposition of other interests, and consociation *via* a roughly equalised formal parity could improve the climate for social partnership or even for improved relationships in a Sturzian sense.[25]

[23] J. Beaufays, *Les Partis Catholiques en Belgique et aux Pays-Bas 1918–58*, Brussels, 1973; F. Spotts; R. Leonardi and D. A. Westman; T. Godechot; and A. Lijphart, *op. cit.*
[24] A. Martinelli and T. Treu in J. P. Windmuller and A. Gladstone, eds., *Employers' Associations and Industrial Relations*, Clarendon, Oxford, 1984; J. Kerkhofs, *The Church in Belgium*, Brussels, 1982; J. Beaufays; F. Spotts; and R. Leonardi and D. A. Westman, *op. cit.*
[25] D. Gladdish in V. Bogdanor, *op. cit.*, J. Hayward, *Private Interests and Public Policy*, the French Economic and Social Council, London, 1966, J. P. Windmuller, *Labour Relations in The Netherlands*, Ithaca, New York, 1969.

Secondly, allied social movements. It is important to realise that the Christian Democratic parties were flanked by often sizable Catholic socio-economic movements which often predated them and made largely separate impacts on political economy. Catholic agricultural organisations were providing educational, co-operative and community activities for large numbers of small farmers. Catholic initiatives were evident in industrial co-operatives in Italy, and in family associations almost everywhere. Catholic (and other Christian) employers tended to represent a relatively socially conscious element of the *patronat*, for example in France and the Netherlands.[26]

The Catholic labour movement was significant. In the Low Countries this organised more workers than the socialists: in France, over one million; in Italy, between two and two and a half million. Catholic trade unionism was pro-democracy and anti-Communist. It engaged in competitive co-operation with a West European socialism which it saw as still trapped into a secularist, anti-clerical sub-culture, too *étatiste*, theoretically Marxist, and in the jargon 'economistic' (though such factors would change). The Catholic trade unions emphasised social solidarity, the family, redistribution, quality of life and work issues, worker participation. They supported socio-economic compacts with government and tended to be moderate, though with a militant edge which increased. During this period they were mostly, but by no means always, critical allies of Christian Democracy or constituents of its substantial left-wings, thereby deploying a 'social' influence on the political economy of co-operation out of proportion to their size.[27]

Finally, the wider Catholic culture. Concepts, symbols and practices based directly on religion were important. Interpretations restricted to electoral centrism, political strategy, anti-Communism, corporate intermediation etc., miss out badly here. Between the 1940s and the 1960s, what Whyte calls a peak point in Catholic power co-existed with a high Catholic culture. The thinking of Maritain, Pesch, Sturzo, Nell Breuning, Dossetti, Mounier, De Lubac, Lebret, the philosophical currents associated with Blondel, Scheler, Gilson, Marcel, a hubble-bubble of neo-Thomism, phenomenology or Christian existentialism, the reviews *Esprit* and *Cronache Sociali*, and leading literary figures including Péguy, Mauriac, Dawson, Bernanos, Chesterton, along with near-neighbours like Simone Weil and Berdyaev, were exerting a widespread influence. Certain concepts were ubiquitous: 'the human person', *une économie personnaliste et communautaire*, 'Christian humanism' or *humanisme intégral*, the title of Jacques Maritain's influential book.[28]

[26] J. H. Whyte, *Catholics in Western Democracies*, Dublin, 1981; R. Leonardi and D. A. Westman; J. Hayward, and W. van Woorden in J. P. Windmuller and A. Gladstone, *op. cit.*

[27] V. R. Lorwin, *The French Labor Movement*, 1954, and D. L. Horowitz, *The Italian Labor Movement*, both Cambridge, Mass;, 1963; G. Adam, *La C.F.T.C.*, Paris, 1964; M. F. Fogarty; R. Leonardi and D. A. Westman; and E. Callot, *op. cit.*

[28] J. H. Whyte even claims, questionably, 'a more influential role .. than ever *before* or since', *op. cit.*, p. 95 (my emphasis).

58

Behind all this lay the directly religious world. Some leading ecclesiastics were liberalising influences: Suhard and Liénart in France, Cardijn in Belgium, Koenig in Austria, Montini and Lercaro in Italy. A range of practices, pilgrimages and processions, retreats, Rosary recitations, bible groups, gave a sense of meaning to those involved through the various movements, climaxing in what was for Catholics the focal communitarian act, the Mass. In wider terms, the system was two-edged, with elements of clericalism, hubris, cosy introversion, even back-scratching *clientelismo*; yet also of outreach, as in projects for social justice expressed in humanistic terms or in the rhetoric of *témoignage* or *engagement*. The mediative political style and ideas of an Aldo Moro, perhaps, typified much of this culture.[29]

The important thing is that the typical *militant* or Christian Democrat cannot be understood without reference to his or her many linkages within this world: sermons, liturgies, bishops and priests, associations, sodalities, informal groups, often on a European or international scale. Formative experiences, letters, reading habits, modes of expression, memberships, conferences, contacts and networks, friendships, attest to its strong influence.[30]

It should be clear that my explanatory model posits causal flows between three factors. These interactions further underpinned or complemented Christian Democracy and its co-operativist roles. Thus, the social movements both recruited from and widened the cross-sectional base, while influence flowed from them to Christian Democratic politics and, perhaps, less markedly, back again. An original cross-sectionalism delivered voting phalanxes which were then reinforced, though not necessarily diversified, by the attractions of Christian Democracy's political centrism and by its *clientelismo*.[31] As for the religious base, this was far from being autonomous. For example, the class structure of Catholicism played back, sociologically, on to its religious culture. But my interpretation does give this last factor a distinctive and considerable weight. It was this which provided most of both the cross-sectional vote and the social movements' memberships, plus the urge to make cross-sectionalism inter-active, plus most of the cement that bound all the elements together, plus, not least, the social ethos.

[29] For useful insights see R. W. Rauch, *Politics and Belief in Contemporary France*, The Hague, 1972, and J. M. Mayeur, *Des Partis Catholiques à la démocratie chrétienne*, A. Colin, Paris, 1980; Aldo Moro, *Scritti e discorsi, 1940–76*, Cinque Lune, Rome, 1982–86; and G. Pallotta, *Aldo Moro, L'uomo, la vita, le idee*, Massimo, Milan, 1978.

[30] See for example R. Poidevin on R. Schuman, P. Scoppola on De Gasperi, G. Pallotta on Moro, and J. Zirnheld, *op. cit.*

[31] J. P. Windmuller, *Labour Relations in The Netherlands*; R. Pasquini in P. Lange and S. Tarrow; and R. Leonardi and D. A. Westman, *op. cit.*

Appraisal and subsequent developments

Twenty-five years later, what sort of evaluation is possible?

Clearly, the 1940s–1960s brand of reformed capitalism fell a long way short, particularly of Catholic social ideals. The system still harboured severe obstacles to community, power-sharing and justice for the poor. Tendencies towards the atomisation, commercialisation or dehumanisation of much of social life remained strong. Power remained too concentrated. The unemployed, immigrants and refugees, those at the bottom of the heap, were helped too little. On the other hand, there were advances in personal and political freedoms, European reconciliation, steady economic growth and, as I have suggested, in the political economy of co-operation.

One might ask, counter-factually, who else could have done this? Across Europe as a whole recognition has to be given to the social democratic route in Scandinavia. Within the Six, however, alternatives would be hard to seek. Such cross-sectionalism and such a culture of economic and political co-operativism were not readily available from elsewhere. On the evidence of history, a straight right-left conflict could have been disastrous. A conservative, economic-liberal régime would have failed the social test. In a régime with democratic socialists as leaders, not just coalition allies as in Austria and the Low Countries, a business-market success would have been less likely. At least during this period, the leading West European socialist parties suffered from mixtures of narrow constituencies, ideological constraints and ambivalences towards a mixed economy.

After the 1960s, of course, the conjuncture I have described came unstuck. Many of the forces unleashed in the 1970s and 1980s burst the bounds of what had been manageable previously. The overstretching of the public sectors: OPEC: the explosion of third world debt: the accelerating magnitudes and volatilities of international trade and financial markets: the environmental factor: the onrush of Reagonomics and Thatchernomics—all would have been hard to tackle even if the resources discussed in this paper had remained intact.

In fact, for different reasons, there was a parallel decline in Christian Democracy. From the 1960s this suffered one blow after another: the collapse of its French embodiment, the M.R.P.; an exodus of working-class Catholics particularly in Germany; a widening distance from the Church following Vatican 2; an increasing secularisation among both supporters and leaders; a loss of impetus after long periods of power. After all this, the spirit could not be the same even where the body still waxed prosperous, as in Italy and Germany. Sturzo's model ship became still harder to recognise as clerics and celebrations no longer attended its launchings, as Catholic miners or factory workers took to the boats, as reformist inspirationalism ran down in both engine room and cabins. With some exceptions, a trend towards moderate conservatism (though not the

60

New Right) took over. Of the earlier socio-reconstructive aims, only the solid Europeanism remained a constant. At the same time, partly reflecting changing currents and controversies within the Church, there was fragmentation in the Catholic social movements.[32]

All this was partially offset by some new manifestations. Two of these bucked the conservative trend in Christian Democracy. In the Netherlands, Catholics and Protestants joined to form the C.D.A. Both influences were evident in the C.D.A.'s intellectual energy and its basic principles of 'justice, differentiated responsibility, solidarity and stewardship'. In Flanders another restatement has emerged, 'social personalism', more characteristically Catholic (and, perhaps, Flemish) in that it groups 'justice' and 'responsibility' under an accentuated 'solidarity' with overtones of conviviality as well as sober restraint. Other tendencies migrated across to different labels or organisational auspices, notably the (still largely Catholic led) French trade union organisation, the C.F.D.T. This union restated 'left Catholic social humanism' with a wide socio-political and economic programme, showed some syndicalist vigour, and developed a thrust towards influencing the Socialist party, associated for a time with Jacques Delors. Such tendencies rejected technical 'economism' and individualism. They favoured 'practices' in a MacIntyrean sense, or the dynamics of human capacities for enjoying, creating and communing.[33]

Official Catholic thought was still reiterating, and to some extent liberalising, the same tradition, from John XXIII through Vatican 2 to Paul VI. For all the controversies of his papacy, John Paul II's social teachings, taken as a whole, have fully maintained the communitarian critique of contemporary capitalism (though the term 'solidarity' itself has, perhaps, been overstretched by the Polish pope). Bishops' conferences around Europe have contributed in similar vein. A militancy for anti-poverty has swept some of the religious orders worldwide, notably the Jesuits. The U.S. Catholic bishops' extended critique of the American political economy, which caused much controversy there and, on the economic right, indignation, has been widely discussed.[34]

[32] R. E. M. Irving, *Christian Democracy in France*, Allen and Unwin, London, 1973; G. Baum and J. Coleman, eds., *The Church and Christian Democracy*, T. Clark, Edinburgh, 1987; E. Callot, R. Papini and J. M. Mayeur, *op. cit.*, G. Pridham, *Christian Democracy in West Germany*, Croom Helm, London, 1977; H. Bakvis, *Catholic Power in the Netherlands*, Queen's University, McGill, 1981; A. Kalaydjiaan and H. Portelli, eds., *Les Démocrates-Chrétiens et l'économie sociale de marché*, Economica, Paris, 1988. The trend was shown by the European People's Party's admission of parties with very different backgrounds from Scandinavia, Spain and Greece, the right-wing international linkages of the German and Austrian parties, and repeated efforts to admit the British Conservatives.

[33] 'Programme of Basic Principles', C.D.A, The Hague; K. Gladdish, *Governing from the Centre, Politics and Policy Making in The Netherlands*, C. Hunt, London, 1990; G. Dierickx, 'Christian Democracy and its ideological rivals', ECPR workshop on Christian Democracy, Limerick, 1992; CEPESS, Forum 2000, Brussels, 1990; R. Mouriaux in M. Kesselman, ed., *The French Workers' Movement*, Allen and Unwin, London, 1984.

[34] B. Davies and M. Walsh, eds., *Proclaiming Justice and Peace, documents from John 23 to John Paul 2*, Collins, London, 1991. U.S. Catholic Bishops, 'Economic Justice for All,

61

Across communitarian thinking as a whole, however, both religious and secular, two major weaknesses could be detected. First, it was still highly diasporised. If links were made between Catholic and some Protestant (and other religious) communitarian streams, those with secular ones were seldom recognised by either side. Some secular thinkers were going beyond a 'thin' version which merely contested thinkers like Rawls, well beyond a mere admission of the community factor's empirical importance. They were exploring the diagnostic and normative implications of local, work or more particularly civic community. But the overlaps were neglected between the religious streams and, for example, Mumford, Arendt, Myrdal, or the tradition of ethical socialism derived from Tawney, or, among more recent theorists, Walzer, Bellah, Hirschman, Nussbaum, Rosenvallon, or in this country Crick, Hirst, Marquand.[35]

The second weakness, a lack of diagnostic and prescriptive follow-up, equally affected both the religious and the secular streams. It should have been clear that a new phase of economic community building would differ from the 1940s–1960s one. Much moderation could then be leveraged via class solidiarities, mass syndics, deferential memberships. But now more of it would have to be teased out from individual economic operators, consumers, investors. Interclassism would face bigger tests. To incorporate a bottom 20 per cent which was fragmented, cut-off, unheard, would be different from raising up a palpable, articulated 50 per cent or 60 per cent. In the 1940s–1960s, institutions for consociation could largely focus at firm, industry or national levels. If a gap in contact or civic responsiveness existed, the answer appeared simple: bring the key people together in another bridge-building body. But now local, regional and European dimensions would have to be added. More fundamentally, it was 'structural' obstacles to public co-operation that would need treatment: those arising from excess volatility, fragmentation, secrecy, anonymity, background social divisions.

Some contemporary lessons

What lessons emerged for our contemporary predicament?

The obstacles look daunting. Who is going to spearhead anything like the syndrome of the 1940s–1960s? What votes, organisations, parties

---

Catholic social teaching and the U.S. economy, 1986', in T. M. Gannon, ed., *The Catholic Challenge to the American Economy*, Macmillan, New York, 1987.

[35] M. Walzer, *Spheres of Justice*, Basic Books, New York, 1983; R. N. Bellah *et al.*, *Habits of the Heart*, University of California, Berkeley, 1985, and *The Good Society*, Alfred A. Knopf, New York, 1991; A. O. Hirschman, *Shifting Involvements*, Robertson, Oxford, 1982; P. Rosenvallon in J. Keane, ed., *Civil Society and the State*, Verso, London, 1988; B. Crick, *In Defence of Politics*, Pelican, London, 1964, P. Q. Hirst, *Representative Democracy and its Limits*, Polity, Cambridge, 1990; D. Marquand, *The Unprincipled Society*, Jonathan Cape, London, 1988.

could they rely on? If something comparable emerges, it would start with long hard thought, research, an intellectual-ethical coalition to unite the dispersed communitarian streams. Its chances would then depend on popular moods, demonstrative events, maybe catalytic crises. Among forces to be overcome not the least is a New Right individualism still so strong that its sway extends to most of the left, 'old', 'new', or 'revisionist'. Yet in part a cyclical interpretation of history comes to the rescue, in part gut conviction. The former implies that a reaction is more likely than not, eventually; perhaps more so in Britain precisely because here regressive capitalism *plus* the New Right have wrought the most havoc. As for conviction, a model might be Jacques Maritain's seminal book, *Humanisme Intégral*, written in 1936 just when, or precisely *because*, the chances for personalist communitarianism in Europe appeared bleaker than for many previous decades.

I conclude with three thoughts relating to communitarian rethinking for a system that now requires not technocratic tinkering but fundamental reform, not massage but overhaul.[36]

The first point questions some conventional wisdoms. There is a conventional view across the 'centre' and 'left' in political economy which tells us that essentially what is needed is a sweeping extension of individually orientated rights, freedoms, choices, opportunities, entitlements, empowerments, independences, self-determinations. But a restated communitarianism suggests that this is not radical enough, even that much of it is unreal.

For most of our society, the incantation of rights, freedoms, etc. fails to hit the right targets either for economic recovery or for anti-poverty. Both of these require collaboration, incomes restraint and tempered consumption and borrowing habits from the bulk of citizens (as well as more active statism). Both economic reconstruction and redistribution towards the poor imply a deceleration of the majority cult of acquisition, a shift of individual ambitions towards economic responsibility and social quality. To trumpet a rights-obsessed prospectus to the great mass of people neglects the resource constraints of a shrinking world. It defies the claims of the Third World poor. The aspirations it fuels are likely to be disappointed. The psychological factors it ignores, those relating to envy, boredom, 'positional goods' etc., are likely to backfire upon it. The qualitative human goods it distracts attention from, above all the relational, communitarian ones, imbue it with a certain thinness and occasion a profound sense of loss.

Secondly, a new approach to interclassism, consocation and economic responsibility would have to go deeper than in the 1940s–1960s. Priority would be attached to the creation of a social fabric, a civil society for the economy, to facilitate civic participation, mutual contact, and sensitivity between its leading parts. The structures which split apart social classes

---

[36] These arguments are developed in J. Boswell, *Community & the Economy, op. cit.*

© The Political Quarterly Publishing Co. Ltd. 1993.

and economic sectors, both from one another and from wider public interests, would have to be addressed. One such obstacle is an excessive volatility of financial resources, property forms, even persons and families. Another is a fragmented pattern of interest group representation which also leaves out marginal groups and the unemployed. Another anti-co-operative factor is the opacity and secrecy which shield major interest groups, and a monitoring system of them by mass media, public bodies or pressure groups which is shot through with holes and bias. There is, too, the lack of representative forums to bring together separate groups to discuss public issues across the critical frontiers between sectors.

There are cultural obstacles to be overcome as well. The paradigms of profit maximising, corporate insularity and managerial 'technique' are inadequate for an interdependent, ethically fraught system. Our business and economic cultures need shifting towards a more balanced respons-ibilism.

Thirdly, a restatement of the tradition discussed in this paper would have to go wider into areas of welfare, everyday life and general culture. For example, it would abandon one-sided 'charters of rights' for 'citizens', 'customers', etc. or at least complement these with responsibilities. One slogan would be 'down with sovereignty, our own or anyone else's, long live mutuality'! The criterion of fraternity, a jealous one, often overlaps with more familiar egalitarian and libertarian pursuits, but never without qualifying and always going well beyond them. Thus, 'anti-poverty' is enlarged so as to include isolation or social entrapment as well as in-adequate income. Gross inequalities in the availability of time or ability for social interactions are deplored at least as much as the latter. Forms of personal property are sought which are not only widely diffusable but stable, socially contributive, transparent, neighbourly. Political decentral-isation is interpreted so that even while power is dispersed, ways are found to foster solidarity with wider groupings (e.g. 'long live Scotland, Britain, and Europe!').

The removal of obstacles to mutuality, conviviality and solidarity, also makes for a distinctive agenda. It focuses on those social formations which disconnect persons or groups from one another, and from the social effects of their actions: generational segregation; one-class ghettoes; uncivil, brutalist urban environments; anomic, a-social styles of work, transport and consumption; education and occupational systems which ensure that whole groups remain total strangers through their entire life spans. Although such shifts in emphasis are radical or 'counter-cultural' in one sense, in another sense they would correspond to widely accepted popular meanings which do, however, require considerable efforts to reclaim.

Summary

I have briefly characterised the Catholic communitarian ideology: its core values of power-sharing subsidiarity and justice, with solidarity at the peak; interclassism and economic responsibility as correlates; agnosticism and eclecticism *vis-à-vis* economic doctrines and methods; an intrinsicist co-operativism with economic performance potential. I have claimed that this ideology and the related movements helped Christian Democracy to play a distinctive role in reforming capitalism through a rudimentary political economy of co-operation. This complemented competition and direction with consociative institutions, economic moderation and centrist mediation. A model for the sociological, organisational and religious dynamics behind this achievement has been proposed. Its subsequent decomposition has been briefly discussed, but also signs of persistent or reviving communitarian tendencies, Catholic, other religious and secular.

My final suggestions raise wider issues about an overhaul of capitalism probably in the longer term. Perhaps the biggest implication of the argument is that even balanced economic success, let alone other things, will tend to elude us unless we manage to reinstate decidedly *trans-* or *supra-*economic pursuits related to personalist community. Further, on the evidence of the past, a religious component appears likely to be still indispensable for such pursuits.

WHAT MAKES THE JAPANESE DIFFERENT?

RONALD DORE*

SHEEP come in all shapes and sizes. So do goats. In fact some sheep look like goats, and vice versa. But as biological systems they are distinct; they won't interbreed. Shoats and geep don't exist.

Are capitalisms like that? Is it true that there are different types of capitalism, and that the differences between them are systemic, i.e., are differences in institutions or patterns of behaviour, sufficiently integrated that institutional borrowing from one to the other is difficult if not impossible? Specifically, does it make sense to talk, as increasingly one hears people talking, particularly after Michel Albert's recent book,[1] about 'German-Japanese capitalism' and 'Anglo-Saxon capitalism'? I hope one day to give a fairly confident answer to that question, but for the moment, Germany is being discussed elsewhere in this volume. I shall confine myself to differences between the US and the UK on the one hand, and Japan on the other. How 'systemic' are they?

The social construction of 'the firm'

A good way to approach this question is to start with a rough classification of the variety of ways in which, currently, people of various persuasions and nationality and social situations view the nature of the private-sector business firm in capitalist societies. Broadly, one can distinguish four major positions. One may call them the property view, the entity/community view (two sub-versions), and the arena view.

The property view is the dominant one among business practitioners in the Anglo-Saxon world. It is represented, for instance, in the reigning assumptions underlying the Cadbury report on company governance. The key assumption is that the legal situation, as set out in the Companies Act, represents social reality. A company is an entity set up by its members to further their own material interest; the managers are their agents with a duty to give priority to that shareholder interest, and the careful buying of the best labour they can as cheaply as they can is as much part of their duty as getting the best bargain out of their suppliers of raw materials. To be sure, the analogy cannot be quite exact, because the people who provide

---

* Professor Dore is currently engaged on research at the Centre for Economic Performance at the London School of Economics, and at the Massachusetts Institute of Technology.

[1] M. Albert, *Capitalisme contre capitalisme*, Editions Seuil, Paris, 1991.

the labour have passions and sentiments and respond differentially to different approaches, unlike, say, the people who supply molybdium. Hence, policies of 'worker involvement', paternalistic welfare policies, premium wages over and above market 'going rates'—all of these tactics may be permissible, provided that these are 'manipulations' designed to yield better value for money in the purchase of labour.

The entity/community view sees the company, by contrast, as something like a nation. Company chairmen talk about 'the future of our great company' much as presidents and kings talk about 'our nation's future'. Two things are involved. One is that the company is, as it were, reified. It is seen as an entity which transcends the participating work life of the individuals involved in it. Secondly, that entity is at any one time concretely embodied in a particular set of people who, as in a nation, constitute a community, tied together by bonds of mutual interest in the community's fate, obligations of co-operation and trust, the sharing of similar risks. The boundaries of that community can vary. it may be limited to the group of senior managers, or senior and middle managers, or it may be extended to the whole body of people who work in the firm, blue collar and white collar. The distinction is important enough to need labels for future reference: *the managerial community view* and *the employee community view*. The latter, the view that the firm is a 'community of people', to use the Pope's phrase in his recent encyclical[2] (don't get too euphoric about the collapse of communism meaning the triumph of capitalism), implies that the shareholders are just one of the groups of outsiders who have to be taken into account for the community to survive and prosper.

The arena view is one favoured among academic analysts—professional economists, business school teachers, etc. The firm is seen as an arena in which individuals or groups of individuals (e.g. managers, skilled workers, suppliers—groups usually referred to as stakeholders) make, often implicit, contracts of various kinds. Firm organisation can indeed be 'dissolved' into a network of contracts; productive activities are pursued as the fulfilment of bargains motivated exclusively by individual self-interest. Principal-agent theory, now a substantial body of economic writing, can be fitted into either the property view or the stakeholder-arena view; sometimes it may be not incompatible with the managerial community view, but never with the employee-community view.

National contrasts

To summarise the contrasts: in the US and the UK, the property view dominates, with some deviation in both countries—though to a somewhat greater extent in the US—towards the managerial community view. The

[2] *Centesimus Annus*, 1991.

67

dominant conception in Japan corresponds to the employee community view, i.e., the employee version of the entity/community view.

Why does one make these judgments? What are the behavioural manifestations of the imputed differing underlying views?

Listen, somebody told me once, to a company chairman addressing shareholders at an annual general meeting. In the US and UK, he's likely to talk about 'your firm, ladies and gentlemen, over the last year . . .'. His Japanese counterpart (though likely to have far less in the way of share and stock options) is much more likely to talk about 'our firm'. But the evidence from behaviour is far more complex and comprehensive than that. Let me list some features in summary form.

The employment relation

1. Employees in large Japanese firms, both blue collar and white collar, are not people who have applied for, and been given, 'jobs' in the firm; they are people who—at a very early age, usually as soon as they leave school or university—have successfully applied to 'become members' of a firm. Membership means that they can have the expectation (sufficiently often fulfilled for it to be a very confident expectation) that they will not just do jobs but make a career in the firm. This pattern of employment, in the US and the UK, is rare, especially in the private sector. It is confined principally to: the armed forces of both countries; the pre-Thatcher UK civil service and pockets (e.g. the State Department) of the US civil service; and the managerial ranks of those private sector companies which deviate most towards the 'managerial community view': viz. Shell, Unilever, Phillips, IBM, Hewlett Packard, etc.

2. It is consequently standard practice in Japanese firms for recruitment selection to be focused, not so much on specific vocational capacities, as on personal qualities, general intelligence and learning ability, for blue collar and routine manual workers as well as, if not quite as much as, for managerial workers. The process can be quite expensively vigorous. Such selection methods are confined to the very limited managerial segments listed above in the US and UK.

3. In Japan the individual's identification with the firm bred by this 'lifetime commitment' is such as to make it unthinkable that, say, a senior manager with a career in Hitachi could move into a comparable position in a directly competing firm like Toshiba. It would be like a captured British officer joining the German army. He might join a steel firm, but, if he was a senior manager, only with Hitachi's blessing. Once, it is said, the UK banking world was rather similar. A Barclays manager would never move to Midland. Perhaps one needs to draw a distinction, though, between the more institutionalised and quite stable, collectivist communitarianism of the contemporary Japanese firm, and the British bank case which might be interpreted as the survival of more paternalistic versions of the 'firm as family'. Even those survivals succumbed, in the end, to the determined

© The Political Quarterly Publishing Co. Ltd. 1993.

onslaught in the 1980s of the reinvigorated property view, laced perhaps with the arena view. In the capitalist arenas, all contracts are one-off. An individual's involvement in the contract-making arena of one firm should not preclude his taking off and entering a different arena.

Indeed, those loyalty, paternalistic duty etc., survivals were under *direct* attack as impediments to efficiency—thanks to the ideological hegemony exercised by the ineffable exponents of a rigid neo-classical economics. But more of this in the final section.

4. A UK, and *a fortiori* a US, chief executive can expect an income from salary, stock options and bonuses, tens or even hundreds of times larger than the average salary in his firm if he has served his shareholder principals well, keeping up dividend earnings and share prices by efficiency, including the efficient holding down of wage costs. A Japanese chief executive in any of the large quoted companies can expect a multiple barely into two figures, only a little more than the other directors from whose ranks he has been promoted, as the apogee of his career. This is almost exactly the same, and by the same criteria, as the way in which permanent secretaries are promoted from under-secretaries in the British civil service. The salary differences are similar. The relationship of the levels of income inequality within the firm to the sense of the firm as community hardly needs pointing out.

5. Labour and trade unions in the US/UK try to bring together all the people offering the same occupational skills in the market, because it is supposed to be the market that fixes their rewards. In Japan they bring together, in enterprise unions, all the people who have committed their future to membership in a particular firm. Their function is (a) to monitor the possibility of unfair treatment of individuals at lower levels of the hierarchy (juniors on managerial career tracks as well as blue collars), (b) in wage bargaining, to represent the interest those furthest from the centres of power have in getting more jam today, as against the tendency of those more responsible people at the top to be more conscious of competing obligations to banks and shareholders, and to want to invest more to gain more jam tomorrow.

6. A Japanese firm's training investments enhance the firm community's pool of skills. In the US and the UK, skills are individual properties. Acquired in one firm, their owner frequently takes them to another. Silicon Valley would not exist without the skill/enterprise spin-off from Intel, TI, Hewlett Packard, IBM, etc.

Enterprise behaviour

It is easy to see how all these different employment institutions breed, are bred by, imply, are congruent with, on the one hand the property view, and on the other hand the employee community view of the firm. There are eight equally characteristic differences in the way firms are managed. First, US/UK managers measure performance above all by return on investment over

69

a relatively short time-frame; Japanese managers by increase in market share. Second (does one need to say, after all the British debate about short-termism?), Japanese firms have a much greater capacity to invest for the long term, if necessary foregoing, thereby, immediate profits.

Third, US/UK managers seek to maintain dividend payments in order to maintain share-values in the depth of a recession (and may even draw down reserves in order to do so) while they are vigorously pruning pay-rolls or 'letting staff go'. Japanese managers will cut dividends for several periods before they resort to the traumatic experience of forced redundancies—and that only after they have been through the preceding stages of managerial pay-cuts, voluntary early retirement, outposting of staff to related companies, etc. Fourth, Japanese firms rely a good deal more on the co-operation of other firms in order to produce their final goods and services. The wholesale:retail sales ratio (about 4:1) is about double Britain's, partly for that reason. (Extra layers in the distribution system account for the other part.) These trading relations between firms are also characteristically different from those in Anglo-Saxon countries.

I said earlier that everybody recognises to some degree that the people who sell a firm labour are different from the people who sell the firm molybdium, in that their passions and sentiments, their capacity for resentment or loyalty have to be taken into account when dealing with them. Japanese managers assume that the sellers of molydium *also* have to be treated in the same way.

The British or American businessman is apt to think that the efficiency of his business depends on his always keeping an eagle eye open for trends in the market. He should always be comparing the deal he is getting from a particular supplier with what he could get elsewhere—and switch without compunction if he finds a better combination of quality and price. The Japanese, by contrast, compunct. Trading relations are seen as generating mutual obligations, and as long as the supplier is fulfilling *his* obligations, 'genuinely and sincerely doing his best' to maintain quality and delivery times, to sink capital in the relationship in order to speed up the joint development of new products, to co-operate in cost-cutting when the market turns down, etc., he has a right not to be ditched just because, perhaps for circumstances beyond his control, another supplier offers a better deal. A list of the sixty-odd members of Toyota's first-line suppliers' club in 1990 has only two or three names not there in 1970, and only two or three of the names which figured in the earlier list have now dis-appeared.

Fifth, first claims on a bankrupt firm's assets are held by banks in the US and UK. Japanese courts give employee wage and redundancy payment claims priority over banks' fixed or floating charges. Sixth, in nothing is the divergence of 'views of the firm' better exemplified than in the practice and regulation of mergers and takeovers. Agreed mergers, to achieve economies by rationalising production, better coordination of related business, better control over markets, etc. occur in all three societies, though a little less often in Japan. How can one explain the difference? To some extent, clearly, in terms of dominant views of the firm.

Such mergers are most obviously compatible with the property view of the firm; if they can be shown to enhance shareholder value, that is the only criterion that counts; the merger should go ahead. Frequently the shareholders have a direct say; the shareholders of at least one of the companies involved can judge whether the merger will be in their interests or not, since the form a merger takes usually involves company A taking over company B, and B's shareholders can decide to sell or not to sell their shares. Alternatively they can take a swap for newly issued A shares, or not.

In the US and UK regime, dominated by an extreme form of the property view, a lot of mergers are not, in any case, aimed at much actual integration of production. They are the product of the sale and purchases by financially expert managers who handle large quantities of shareholders' funds and add to or dispose of a portfolio of production units, over which they exercise control only by regular scrutiny of various financial indicators and the approval or non-approval of investment plans—the case of the pure 'holding company' or of the conglomerate which is a holding company in anything but name. The dominance of such company structures in the US and the UK contrasts with their absence in Japan. Indeed, holding companies proper were banned under the postwar, American-inspired company legislation, and although most other anti-trust provisions introduced then have been modified or abandoned, this one has not.

Mergers take on a different aspect when they are not portfolio transactions but a real fusing of production activities—and especially if there is any deviation towards the managerial community view of the firm. Problems arise. The 'rationalisation' that follows a merger may well mean that some managers may have to be 'let go'. Only one of two present managing directors and chairmen can have the same position in the new firm; somebody is going to be disappointed, and the prospective disappointees may well be in a position to halt the merger. Shift even further to the Japanese employee community view and the uneven distribution of gains and losses becomes much greater. Whole plants may be shut down in the rationalisation at which the merger aims.

It is not only jobs and power distributions which are shaken up; there is also a confusion of loyalties. This can happen even with long-tradition ex-family firms in the UK—witness the uneasy merger of Austin and Morris in BL. But the difficulties are much magnified in a society where the employee-community view of the firm predominates as in Japan. Fuji Steel and Yawata Steel merged with the blessings of MITI into New Japan Steel at the beginning of the 1970s. Still, one is told, every manager over 45 knows who are the ex-Fuji and who the ex-Yawata men, scrutinises appointments suspiciously to make sure that the 'other side' is not gaining too much, and finds it easier to talk freely to his own kind. The stories are

71

doubtless exaggerated, but it is generally acknowledged that the strong sense of identification with the firm bred in the employee-community atmosphere implies a strong insider/outsider sense which acts as a serious deterrent to mergers. Try making a Tottsenal team by merging Tottenham Hotspur and Arsenal.

Seventh, the differences among the countries are magnified as soon as one moves from agreed mergers to hostile takeovers. These are accepted practice in the US and the UK. They are viewed with distaste and occur rarely in Japan.

There are, to be sure, differences in this regard between the US and the UK. Highly leveraged takeovers—financed by junk bonds—have not been as common in the latter as in the former, particularly in the Reagan years, the heyday of Boeskie and Boone Pickens. The difference lies largely in the more conscientious adherence to a strict property view in Britain, thanks to the regulations formulated by the non-statutory Takeover Panel and that Panel's policing of those regulations. The fundamental principle underlying those regulations are:

takeovers are justified if they will lead to a better use of the assets held by the taken-over company because they thereby enhance shareholder value;

shareholders themselves are the best judges of that, and the decision (to swap their shares for shares of the new company or to take a price for them which represents that prospective 'value enhancement') must lie with them;

and in that regard, all shareholders should be treated equally, all having the same options, and be given an equal amount of information on which to base their choices and adequate time to consider it.

Most of the Takeover Panel's rules are concerned to ensure the third principle: such, for example, are the requirements that any single shareholder's acquisition of a certain percentage of shares should be made public, delays to allow managers of threatened companies to provide the information for shareholders by which they alone can defend their management record, and so on.

The much rougher, tougher American scene may be said to differ in the following respects. First, the controls on insider dealing are less effective—both the external legal sanctions and the 'gentleman's honour' internal sanctions. There are fewer ambiguous 'gents', more shameless buccaneers. Hence there is more frequent and effective manipulation of stock prices to facilitate mergers by arbitrageurs. Secondly, there are more gullible risk-taking investors in US financial markets, willing to invest in the junk bonds which have, since 1980, financed a lot of take-over activity. And thirdly, as is exemplified in the fact that a large number of take-overs have been leveraged buy-outs by existing management teams, there is a greater and more readily condoned tendency in the US to deviate from a strict property view towards a managerial community view of the firm.

But in both societies the dominant principle of judgment is investor protection—protection of the capital-owner's right to make up his own mind as to how he can best get the maximum return on his capital. The only other principle invoked is a particular public good—the preservation of market competition, which is secured by, for example, British provisions which allow reference of takeover bids to the Monopolies and Mergers Commission.

The contrast with a Japan dominated by the employee community view could not be more marked. As a Japanese economics dictionary says: 'the idea of taking over a firm simply by the power of money seems too "dry" [the adopted English word, used in contemporary Japanese to mean coldly calculating, oblivious to human feeling] to us Japanese, and takeovers rarely happen'.[3] The objections are the same as the objections to agreed mergers mentioned above—raised to a higher power.

That is not to say that both Japanese and foreigners do not occasionally try, and the Japanese stock exchange has much the same set of rules governing takeovers as the US. Most of the Japanese instances involve not major firms but relatively small quoted companies which are made the target of some crooked greenmailer, concerned only to get enough shares to enable him to make enough trouble that the target company buys back the shares—or gets its friends to buy them, rather—at a premium. The most famous case in recent times involves the missionary activities of T. Boone Pickens, one of the hero buccaneers of the Reagan 1980s, who acquired from a Japanese failed greenmailer a sizable packet of shares in one of Toyota's supplier companies, Koito. He used, it subsequently transpired, money borrowed from the same greenmailer who apparently hoped to achieve what his own efforts had failed to achieve, by wielding the political clout at the command of an American backed by American government charges that Japan was a conspiratorially closed society. T. Boone Pickens was seen off. His apparent right under Japanese company law to nominate directors was circumvented as Koito's banks and related firms co-operated first to dilute the share ownership, and in the end to consolidate ownership of the other shares in such a way that Koito could no longer be a quoted company.

Finally, how do companies raise finance for their activities? In all three countries they do this to a large extent out of their earnings, but to a much greater extent in Japan where the employee community view provides extra justification for ploughing back money to secure the long-term future. The most interesting difference arises with respect to issuing new equity. When a company needs more funds, and its managers think that— given interest rates, and the availability of different kinds of funds and the kind of quotation they currently enjoy in the market—they could best raise it as risk capital, how does it go about issuing the shares? In Britain the procedure most closely exemplifies property view assumptions. Company law gives existing shareholders pre-emption rights. Through transactions

---

[3] Nikkei Shimbun, *Hai-tekku jiten*, 1986, entry TOB.

on the stock market, the identity of 'members of the company' may actually change from minute to minute, but the mid-nineteenth century paradigm of the joint stock company still embodied in British company law, sees them as a relatively stable group of like-minded people who have come together in support of a particular venture. And it remains true that, in spite of the growth of the stock market, at any one time the 'members' of the company constitute a clearly defined set of people. Pre-emption rights mean that that set of people has the first right of refusal when new shares are being issued. The standard practice is a 'rights issue'—for every x shares they hold, shareholders are entitled to buy y new shares at z price.

In the US, however, pre-emption rights count for very little. Companies frequently place a big block of new shares with a securities company which then sells them on to investors who may or may not be existing shareholders. In the words of one commentator[4] this pattern of 'vendor placings' or 'bought deals' is 'faster and cheaper for the company, the big company men claim. This poses a paradox. How can a procedure be good for the company if it is not good for the shareholders who own the company?'

Because, the answer is, the property view gives way somewhat in the United States—more so than in the UK—*either* to the entity/management community view (managers as the responsible carriers of the destiny of the company entity) or to the arena view (managers as one interest group among several, quite reasonably asserting their interests *vis-á-vis* shareholders). The latter, of course, is a reformulation of the argument about 'the divorce of ownership from control' set off by Berle and Means in the 1930s, but the distinction between it—the arena view, which seems to fit the reality of, say, RJRNabisco—and the entity/managerial community view—which seems to fit rather better the situation in an IBM or a DEC—is not unimportant.

The contrast of both with Japan is very considerable. To start with, Japanese firms have traditionally been most inclined to turn to banks for long-term loans. Managers thereby put the firm in the power of other managers very like themselves (often from the same universities) who can be persuaded of their projects *in the same terms as they justify them to themselves*. They do not need to resort to smart sales talk designed for the gullible anonymous investor—of the kind that makes it worthwhile for every weekend newspaper in Britain to devote several pages to family finance (column after column assessing this smart talk for the benefit of the punters)—one of the clearest manifestations of the sick nature of our casino society.

In Japan the firms which depend on this bank lending are also, usually, holders of the bank's equity. A balanced mutuality of obligation is sought wherever possible. Further, the bank is almost certain to own some of the

---

[4] Michael Brett, *How to read the financial pages*, Hutchison Business Books, London, 1987, p. 115.

74

equity of the firm to which it lends money; so also do the fire and accident insurance companies which do the firm's insurance business, and the life insurance company which offers a special scheme for the company's employees or runs its pension fund. So also do the other major firms which supply it with raw materials, buy its products, or those with which it has joint ventures or strategic tie-ups to develop new lines of business.

By agreements between firms to buy up each other's shares in the market, and by subsequent issues of new shares which have amplified the holdings thus acquired, Japanese firms have built up sizable mutual security cross-holdings. These are very sizable indeed. Most quoted firms have over seventy per cent of their equity locked up in the safes of trading partners who would never unload them, on the stock market or otherwise, without consulting the firm affected. The stock market handbooks list the percentage—on average around 25 per cent—of a company's shares which are floating shares—i.e., shares freely traded in the market without reference to the original issuing firm.

It is partly because the floating shares a raider might lay hands on are scarce that nobody ever gets much of a chance to overcome any traditional inhibitions and acquire a taste for the hostile takeover. And that, in turn, is why Japanese industrial managers do not go first to the stock price pages when they get their newspapers. They in fact can show casual indifference to what the shady manipulations of the security companies happen to be doing to their share prices from day to day. That freedom from the fear of takeover, and ability to contemplate decline in their stock prices for a while provided the growth indicators are good, is one of the reasons why they can spend so much time thinking about, and can so readily commit the necessary funds to, long-term investment.

A system?

There are two ways in which one can talk about these society-wide differences in organisation and behaviour constituting different 'systems' of capitalism. Integration by 'institutional interlock' and integration by 'motivational congruity'. To illustrate the first, let us take the three salient features: the lifelong *versus* the mobile employment relationship; long-term, obligated *versus* auction-market mobile, supplier relations; and patient, long-term committed *versus* mobile, short-terms-returns-sensitive, equity capital.

It is easy to see the way in which, by institutional interlock, the choice on any one of these three dimensions creates a disposition for—or indeed is a precondition for—a parallel choice in the other two dimensions. The fact that employees more or less commit their lives to a company immensely reinforces the employee community view of the firm. This, first makes the firm's reputation of great importance to all employees and so helps to guarantee to a supplier that 'the firm' will not renege on its obligations,

75

© The Political Quarterly Publishing Co. Ltd. 1993.

however frequent the change-over of purchasing managers; and secondly, it similarly reassures cross-shareholding partners that the other side will stick to its obligations to hold capital 'patiently'. Then again, the long-term career calculations of personal interest on the part of lifetime-employees give them the long-term , market-share-oriented business attitudes which made them build up the cross-shareholding patterns in the first place—at the price, be it said, of locking up a lot of their financial assets, making a considerable sacrifice of liquidity. The long-term perspective of the firm also explains why it seems worthwhile to managers to invest in their relation with long-standing suppliers—even at the sacrifice of short-term gains which a switch in suppliers might bring.

What about the other sense of integration—'motivational congruence'? Can one see a consistency of behaviour? Is there, in all these features listed, a similarity in the values which seem to be maximised, in the moral constraints that seem to be obeyed, which would make one say: well, it's just that people brought up in Japanese families and schools *are largely predisposed* to behave in this way, to fit into this kind of institution. People brought up in British or American schools are predisposed to behave the other way and to fit into that other kind of institution. *On average*, that is. One doesn't have to say that no Americans could fit happily into a Japanese-type firm or that no Japanese could fit into the individualistic short-term life of a British company. The range of behavioural predispositions is large in both societies. We are talking only about central tendencies.

Note that I ask about 'behavioural dispositions', avoiding the much more common but protean word 'culture'. Culture usually implies not only the existence of certain behavioural tendencies but also some sort of explanation of their origins in some vaguely-conceived 'tradition'. It is much better, for the present discussion, to leave the question of origins aside, though one might just list some of the features an inquiry into origins would have to consider. These include long-standing traditions of explicit morality like Christianity or Confucianism; long-standing patterns of social relationships (e.g., gift-giving patterns); historical circumstances like the experience of being a pioneering or a late-developing industrialiser, a victor or a defeated nation in the last world war; and, finally, differences in population gene pools. (Whisper it not to anyone susceptible to the charge of being a racist, but if genes determine bone structure and the thickness of stomach walls and the propensity of new-born babies' bottoms to have thirty-day strawberry birth-marks, why shouldn't they also affect the aggressiveness/passivity balance, the deference/self-assertion balance, etc.—even, God forbid, intelligence?)

So what might be the behavioural dispositions involved? The first, a constant theme in all that has been said, that Anglo-Saxons behave in ways designed to keep their options—their freedom of choice—open. Japanese are much more willing to foreclose their options by making long-term commitments. Secondly, in making their choices, Anglo-Saxons give

76

greater weight to their own immediate welfare or that of their family. Japanese are much more likely, by virtue of their long-term commitments, to have diffuse obligations to promote the welfare of others—the other members of firms they have joined, their partners in long-term obligated relationships, etc.

Thirdly, and this is a difference in behavioural dispositions rather more often elevated to an explicit cultural ideal than the previous two: there is a difference in the moral evaluation of different kinds of human activity. In Japan, producing goods and services which enhance the lives of others is good. Spending one's life in the speculative purchase and sale of financial claims is bad. That 'productivist' ethic is far from absent in Anglo-Saxon countries, but, in all the ways described by Wiener in his *British Culture and the Decline of the Industrial Spirit* it has become far more attenuated than in Japan. The direct transition of the gentry to gentlemanly banking rather than to entrepreneurship helped in Britain; the sanctification of time and charity trusts made folk heroes of the Rockefellers and Morgans in the US. In those countries there is a much greater disposition to nod sagely when economists demonstrate that speculation in secondary markets is the way in which the invisible hand ensures that markets get the prices right and that the producers of goods and services get adequate signals on which to base their production decisions. Japanese are more likely to be sceptical and to answer: (a) the proliferation of secondary market goes well beyond what such arguments might justify; (b) even if speculation is a partially beneficial evil in its consequences, it is still an evil in its motivation, and a beneficial evil is not necessarily a necessary evil. It might be better to sacrifice some market efficiency in order not to encourage immorality—not to allow such practices as takeovers which allow bad people like full-time financial manipulators to dominate the fate of good people who are intent on producing valuable goods and services.

The last element—the behavioural disposition to listen to certain kinds of economists—cannot be overlooked as a major factor in maintaining the separateness of the two systems. The dominant school of neo-classical economists—the school that almost totally commands the ideological airspace of universities in the US and the UK, and has a lesser but still highly influential command of journalism and extra-university policy discussion in those countries—is wholly committed to a belief in the desirability of the one, the Anglo-Saxon, way of organising society. ('Desirability' usually means intrinsic moral desirability, though if pressed many economists will fall back on means-end desirability—necessary to produce the valued social end of efficiency.) They are also committed because they believe that efficiency is maximised by the maximum mobility of resources. It is precisely in societies where people always keep their options open—where markets are mobile because people can, from moment to moment choose and rechoose where to spend their time and their money—that resources of labour and capital get allocated to the uses which yield the highest returns.

I commented earlier on the way in which paternalistic survivals in the form of notions of company loyalty were under direct attack in the 1980s as 'rigidities' which impeded the proper functioning of the market. The dominant view propagated by the OECD in the mid-eighties was that a crucial ingredient of Eurosclerosis was this rigidity in the labour market. It was supposed to be because of its much greater labour market flexibility that the US had a much better record of employment-creation and lower unemployment rates than the European economies. (It had lower productivity growth also, and much worse rates of poverty creation—including poverty of those in work—but that was overlooked.)

The dominant economist community held two central agreements as axiomatic. First, the mobility of capital and labour around the market is a prime precondition for economic growth, because it is a necessary pre-condition for allocative efficiency (almost, but not quite, a sufficient as well as a necessary condition—there are also information problems). Secondly, allocative efficiency is either: (i) the only sort of efficiency that counts as a source of economic growth, i.e., that other dimensions of efficiency—for example, the 'production efficiency' that comes from working skilfully and conscientiously and co-operatively to produce high quality goods—can be ignored *per se* because, when it comes down to it, it really resolves itself into the market-efficiency principle of making sure that such qualities reap their just reward—i.e., that wages flexibly fluctuate to equal marginal productivity; or (ii) the only sort of efficiency that can be much affected by policy measures, or at least by the only sort of (market-lubricating) policy measures acceptable in the Hayekian ideological clim-ate of the Anglo-Saxon 1980s; or (iii) the only sort of efficiency which can be satisfactorily quantified, thus permitting the arcane algebraic and econ-ometric manipulations which provide economists with their main pleasure in life, their criterion for professional excellence and their side revenues from, e.g., OECD research commissions (and to hell with criteria of relevance).

Deviant institutional economists have over the years pointed out often enough that the *extreme* rigidities of the German and Japanese labour market do cast just a wee bit of doubt on the assumption that flexible mobility around the labour market is a necessary precondition for growth, and that, maybe, the explanation is to be sought by concentrating on analysis of productive rather than merely allocative efficiency. Their impact on the self-confidence of the neo-classical mainstream has, how-ever, been slight. In 1992 the American National Bureau of Economic Research was still able to mobilise perhaps some 20–30 man/woman-years of effort for a conference in London on 'Social protection and labour market flexibility. Is there a trade-off?'. And it was still possible for the papers to take as axiomatic the assumption that labour market mobility was the road to prosperity. Thus, a comparison of US and German health insurance systems was designed to answer the question: how far does the reportedly frequent unwillingness of American workers to leave their jobs because they would lose health benefits actually lead to greater (inefficiency-producing) job lock than a better (e.g., German-type) health system might produce? The paper did an exhaustive job of squeezing probability significance out of the differences between the insured and the uninsured in the two countries, without ever mentioning—as just possibly relevant to the significance of the whole exercise—that there were massive differences between the two societies in the *overall* level of rigidity/ mobility. The proportion of Americans changing their jobs over the years studied varied (according to admittedly not very believable statistics) from 55 to 66 per cent per annum; the proportion of Germans from two to six per cent.

Locked into systems?

Many people would say: to be sure the Japanese achieve higher levels of efficiency, but, thank you, we can do without such efficiency if the price is the sacrifice of freedom, of the ability to keep one's options open, the ability to reshape one's career by choosing one's own job options instead of submitting to the persuasions of the personnel office, the ability to choose one's own financial future by making one's own choice among the bits of advice offered in the family finance columns, not by being locked into long-term savings and investments. Others would see the advantages of the institutional arrangements of Japanese society but see no possibility of ever adopting them because systems cannot be changed piecemeal. Institutions do not work in the same way when they are torn out of context; the behavioural dispositions which alone make them possible cannot be created overnight.

But that is not necessarily so. It is more complicated than that. The mutual security cross-shareholding in Japan is a creation of the last quarter-century. Lifetime employment three-quarters of a century ago was confined, as in Britain, to the public service and the managerial ranks of a very small number of predominantly commercial and financial firms. In the depression of the mid-1950s, the willingness of large firms to cut out subcontractors and take work in-house was remarked on as a feature of the ruthlessness of Japan's 'dual economy' capitalism.

Piecemeal change does happen. Change in one firm can spread to others. Change in one set of institutionalised practices can induce complementary change in others. Even assumptions about the purpose of life and the most effective and most moral means of achieving those purposes can change. So, even, can fashions in economic theory. The message to be derived from exercises in international comparison like the present one is not that each nation has its own *Gestalt* and never shall diverse *Gestalten* meet. Comparisons broaden one's awareness of the range of options human beings have open to them. Comparisons of systems underline the message; when making institutional changes, be sure you think through how, in relation to other institutions, the innovation fits in.

79

CO-OPERATION AND COMPETITION IN AN INSTITUTIONALISED ECONOMY: THE CASE OF GERMANY

COLIN CROUCH*

THE economy of the post-war Federal Republic of Germany has been variously perceived in Britain as embodying characteristics favoured by the political right (the non-Keynesian, monetarist economy, and some interpretations of the *soziale Marktwirtschaft* or social market economy with the emphasis placed on the market); the centre (the consensus economy of *konzertierte Aktion* or concerted action, and interpretations of the social market stressing balance between social and market); and the left (the economy with integrated trade unions and the social market economy with the emphasis placed on the social, the welfare state). All these accounts are highly self-serving; the German economy being seen as successful, it is useful if one can associate its attributes to one's own preferences. The only exception was perhaps the view taken by those around the Thatcher government, who, despite the monetarism of the Bundesbank, tended rather oddly to share a 'left' view of German economic institutions and therefore drew attention not to its successes, but to its cumbersomeness, the slowness to adapt induced by corporatism and the insistence on a national consensus that included trade unions.

The central argument of this chapter is to claim that there are 'lessons' to be drawn from a study of German economic institutions, but these are not immediately translatable into the preferences of British political parties. And an important part of the learning exercise is how to go about the task of taking policy lessons from another society in the first place. The main offence committed by the various *parti pris* accounts is to see German institutions through British eyes and not in terms of their internal logic and historical development.

For example, that variously interpreted phenomenon, the social market, has a meaning in German economic history that entirely lacks resonance in Britain.[1] The concept was an invention of rightist economic

---

* Colin Crouch, joint editor of *The Political Quarterly*, is a fellow of Trinity College, Oxford. His works include *Industrial Relations and European State Traditions*, Oxford University Press, Oxford, 1993.

[1] M. Welteke, *Theorie und Praxis der sozialen Markwirtschaft*, Campus Verlag, Frankfurt am Main, 1976.

thinkers in the closing years of Hitler's regime. Behind them was a German past of heavily protectionist and cartelised economic policy originating with Bismarck's unification strategy and similarly followed by the Nazi regime. They were now living in a European continent dominated, from occupied France to Soviet Russia and excluding only Switzerland, by oligarchic regimes interfering massively with the allocative mechanisms of the market for state and often military purposes.

Behind them also stood the record of a non-democratic residual welfare state under Bismarck, the doomed attempt to create a compromise between social democracy and the military of the Weimar Republic, and the Nazi regime ferociously hostile to welfare policy except of a militaristic kind. They saw their problem as one of bringing Germany towards greater acceptance of open markets, domestically and internationally, while reassuring the working class that this could embrace a degree of social security and welfare, need not lead to the disruption that had been wrought to the European and American economies by the depression, and therefore need not provoke a turn towards the Soviet model. This is not readily translatable into remedies for the United Kingdom at the end of the 20th century.

A similar point applies to the absence of Keynesian policies during the first two decades of the Bonn Republic and their rather minor role even after the official acknowledgement of their utility in 1967. As Matzner and Streeck[2] have shown, this did not mean that governments and others were left with no policy instruments other than those of the pure market economy, such as monetary regulation. Instead there was an interesting range of instruments of micro-policy, with the state not being the only policy agent. Some of these policies will be discussed below. The central point here is that the lack of Keynesianism has a different meaning in an economy where there are many other policy instruments from one where there are few.

Concerted action has also been much misunderstood. The formal mechanism of *konzertierte Aktion* was a tripartite forum, not unlike, but not perhaps as well developed as, the British National Economic Development Council. Because this was visible and formal, the apparent consensus of German industrial relations was often ascribed to it. Most studies of the institution, however, agree that, after its initial years in the late 1960s and early 1970s, it was of little substantive importance.[3] Indeed, when in 1977 the unions boycotted its meeting to demonstrate their dissatisfaction with certain actions of some employers' associations, not only did the other participants in the forum continue to meet, but not much happened to change the ways of German industrial relations.

[2] E. Matzner and W. Streeck, 'Towards a Socio-Economics of Employment in a Post-Keynesian Economy', in Matzner and Streeck, eds, *Beyond Keynesianism: the Socio-Economics of Production and Full Employment*, Edward Elgar, Aldershot, 1991.

[3] H.-D. Hardes, *Einkommenspolitik in der BRD*, Herder und Herder, Frankfurt-am-Main, 1974.

Ironically, it was during that period, especially 1978 and 1979, that both the Labour Party and the Confederation of British Industry were most enthusiastically commending the German concerted action forum for imitation in Britain.

But, inaccurate though these commendations were, they at least had the merit of locating German consensus-seeking within institutions, rather than attributing it to some disembodied sentiment of consensus-proneness. Consensus might be an outcome of institutional incentives to certain kinds of behaviour, and that outcome may well then feed back as an influence on subsequent behaviour because of the expectations and trust it generates; but it is rarely a pre-condition for behaviour. Aspiration to consensus, or fear of dissensus, might influence behaviour by encouraging people to set up institutions that will then force them to act in certain ways, but that is very different from an already accomplished consensus. This is certainly true of the way in which Germans set about reconstructing their country after 1945. They did not begin with a detailed consensus, since their recent past gave them little basis for trust. What they did have was a desperate fear of failing to achieve it. For most of the past twenty years it has been difficult to persuade interested persons outside Germany that this was not a confident society easily expressing the rosy consensus of a rich country, but rather an anxious one concerned that its democratic institutions might still be fragile. Perhaps events since the unification of 1990 have enabled them to see this more clearly.

I do not want to deny that ideas have their place. But I do want to argue, and to use the German example to argue, that our attention has to be kept firmly on institutions and the incentives to behaviour that they provide. To take a more specific case than the vague idea of consensus: Germans, we are told, often by Germans themselves, have a horror of inflation based on the experience of the Weimar republic, and this explains why they keep their inflation rate so low. But by no means all countries that have had spells of very high inflation develop subsequently such a powerful apparent aversion to the phenomenon. Neither do all low-inflation countries have a similar high inflation past; one thinks primarily of Switzerland. And if it was the experience of the 1920s that has given Germans this aversion, the sentiment ought to be wearing out as memories fade and new generations come into adulthood. Far more worthy of examination is the institution that embodies anti-inflationary sentiment: the Bundesbank. It was itself the result of a determination to avoid inflation; and it remains a symbol of the struggle against it, perhaps reinforcing the relevant values. But the institutional fact of its existence, its autonomy from political intervention and its ability therefore to pursue its clear mandate to sustain the purchasing power of the Deutsche Mark, is more telling than ideas.

Ethics (or values) can be a major influence on behaviour only when they are embodied in institutions. This by itself, however, implies autonomy in institution building: given that a 'determination' to construct institutions with a particular purpose is sufficiently strong among key decision makers, they will be able to do so. In practice the materials available to any one society at a given time are restricted, or at least strongly influenced, by the historical legacy. These institutions are themselves repositories of a legacy of values that are the products of the institutions. It is therefore more accurate to regard policy attempts as having to be content with co-determining the future alongside the legacy of the past. There are perhaps exceptions to this, where such factors as the formation of an entirely new society or a prior episode of institutional destruction produce an historical *tabula rasa*, when institution-builders have a genuine autonomy. This is indeed one common interpretation of the German case, the Hitler period being seen as one of total institutional destruction and sharp discontinuities being perceived between the post-1949 Federal Republic and previous Germanies.[4] However, as I hope to show below, this underestimates the degree of continuity in certain fundamental characteristics in German political economy that reaches back past all the apparent discontinuities of that country's geography and history.

Germany's moral and institutional legacies

We therefore need to approach the German record in terms of institutional legacies and what was made of them. Interestingly, the story turns on the perpetuation of certain archaic qualities in German social and economic organisation which, partly deliberately but partly fortuitously, helped build some extraordinarily adaptive and creative structures.

In his remarkable book, *Social Limits to Growth*, the late Fred Hirsch[5] recalled an argument of (surprisingly) Adam Smith that the market society of capitalism needed an ethical base on which its central mechanisms, such as the idea of respect for contract, could rest, but it could not generate such an ethic itself. It therefore depended on the moral legacy of the pre-capitalist past. Since this legacy could not be replenished by a society based on market relations it constituted, in Hirsch's memorable phrase, 'the depleting moral legacy of capitalism'. By the late 1970s it was beginning to wear very thin. It is a kind of meta-instance of the more general problem of market failure, the inability of market processes to produce public goods. Here it is the market system *qua* system that fails to generate the public goods on which it itself depends. Where Hirsch speaks in moral and ethical terms, I would prefer to speak of 'values as embodied in institutions'. Thus conceived the point can be applied in an interesting way to the idea of German 'archaism'.

[4] Most notably in M. Olson, *The Rise and Decline of Nations: Economic Growth , Stagflation and Social Rigidities*, Yale University Press, New Haven, Conn, 1982, which attributes German economic dynamism to an alleged but quite misconceived total destruction of its institutional continuities during and after World War II.

[5] F. Hirsch, *Social Limits to Growth*, Routledge and Kegan Paul, London, 1977.

W. Fischer published in 1964[6] a fascinating account of how the modern organisation of German business and its relationship to the state feed on the legacy of medieval guild society. The author appreciated the paradox whereby institutions that looked quaint from the perspective of 19th century liberalism looked remarkably apposite in the context of mid-20th century organised capitalism. From here runs a straight line to two central features of contemporary Germany: the organised nature of its business life, and its obsession with the creation of industrial skill. To this we need to add three further points to build up a full model of the distinctiveness of the German economy.

1. the role of the banks is intrinsic to the model, but also ensures that the economy is oriented to achievement and modernisation;

2. the incorporation of labour made the existing model democratic and reduced its tendencies to exclude difficult interests;

3. the Bundesbank has inhibited what might have been protectionist and inward-looking tendencies.

The outcome is a system that reliably reproduces an advanced manufacturing economy with a high capacity for the co-operative production of collective goods and trust relations.

From guilds to organisations

Fischer describes how the transition from pre-industrial to industrial society in Germany, unlike England or France, was achieved without widescale destruction of medieval guild institutions. The Prussian state that built united Germany was itself an economically backward part of Europe and carried such institutions more or less intact into the period of its modernising mission. It encountered similar institutions elsewhere in the German lands. The Hanseatic city states on the Baltic and North Sea coast had their own corporate form of organisation; the southern lands had a Catholic legacy of corporatist forms; in the Rhineland the brief Napoleonic invasion had ironically imposed a French structure of state-appointed *chambres* which Prussia adapted to its own system of more genuinely representative structures. The central import of these institutions was that they embodied the idea of political authority over economic questions being shared between the state as such and representative bodies of the various trades and crafts.

This feature of the Prussian and German state is often lost in the tendency for British observers to see Germany primarily as an example of the strong state and to forget that, in contrast with the French form of the phenomenon, the German model incorporated the idea of representative organisations of trade interests. Not only in practice, but in the theoretical underpinning of Prussian *Staatslehre* provided by Hegel himself, the state

---

[6] W. Fischer, *Unternehmerschaft, Selbstverwaltung und Staat*, Duncker und Humblot, Berlin, 1964.

exists on a prior basis of more immediate social and communal ties, including those of guild and urban community. The misperception is understandable. In the late 19th century it was the state rather than the patchwork of modernised old structures that most differentiated Germany from Britain, although Britain had in a different way many examples of the latter. In the 20th century two world wars and the ghastly extreme state form of Nazi Germany, was wrongly seen by us to be an exaggeration of German forms, whereas in fact in its centralism and *Führerprinzip* it was a contradiction of them. This is not to pretend that Imperial Germany was a benign society, merely to point out that it was not just a state-led one.

We should note that the Prussian model implies a state that is not jealous of its role as the guardian of public decision-making and enforcement. This possibility is neglected in most political theory and practice. Our central political tradition is that of building monarchies out of feudalism, and the obsession is with degrees of centralisation of a 'pure' political power conceived in terms of abstracted rule. But a different unsung tradition developed in the towns of much of medieval Europe, where politics had more to do with the maintenance of an albeit hierarchical community, and where order, welfare and the practice of crafts worked alongside each other to produce a certain view of political power and practice.[7] We find this tradition virtually everywhere north of the line of latifundium plantations in Spain and southern Italy (where little interrupted the rule of rural nobility and towns were little more than dormitories for unfree rural labourers) and west of the second serfdom of eastern Europe (where towns were rarely more than garrisons). The urban tradition was especially important where the mercantile activity or the small scale of national units gave prominence to virtual city states: the Hanseatic towns, Flanders, Denmark, northern Italy.

In England and France, the urban legacy eventually became thoroughly subordinated to national monarchies. In Italy it became compromised with aristocratic takeover, foreign rule and finally a unification of the nation which spread from the latifundium south. In Germany (and the Low Countries) the tradition continued to thrive, being particularly favoured by the retarded growth of the nation state, and (unlike Italy) being built into the activity of the nation-building forces of the mid-19th century.

One key institution that carried Germany through the transition from backwardness to modern industrial organisation was the *Kammer*, essentially the same word as the French *chambre* or the English chamber, as in chamber of commerce, but very different in form and role. *Kammer* existed for both modern factory industry (*Industrie*) and for the workshop-based artisan crafts (*Handwerk*). Membership of them was compulsory for persons wishing to pursue most forms of economic life

---

[7] A. Black, *Guilds and Civil Society in European Political Thought from the Twelfth Century to the Present*, Macmillan, London, 1984.

and their rules and procedures were governed by statute. They did, however, elect their own representatives from among practitioners of the various trades, and made representations to and were consulted by government on matters affecting trade. Some public administration was delegated to them. They had a structure moving from local to national levels through a complex intermediate web of consultation.

Although their precise form has changed, *Kammer* still exist as a central feature of the administration of industry and trade in modern Germany, and they still play that intermediary role linking both the state to trade and different levels of representation of the business world to each other.[8] They are ideally located for the pursuit of those forms of action that so often prove difficult for business groups: the provision of public goods and the pursuit of collective action. They have the power to require firms to share in agreed collective tasks. Also, unlike simple state enforcement of rules, their detailed contacts with and legitimacy among the business community make it likely that their interventions will be acceptable.

From here the general high organisational density of German industry can be explained. Once being part of a system of order that requires co-operation, German businesses find it easy and acceptable to be part of other collective systems. Trade associations and employer organisations not only have very high memberships, they are also able to impose sanctions to punish deviance without firms responding by simply quitting membership. The fact that broadly similar people are involved in running the *Kammer* and the various associations means that the formal positive and negative sanctions available to the *Kammer* can also influence a firm's views of its obligations to voluntary membership associations. These associations in turn create a network of acquaintanceship and face-to-face ties.

The federal structure of modern Germany facilitates this further, as many of the relationships formed by business organisations make use of the regional or *Land* governments. These not only exist at a level more immediate than the ministries of a large European state, but have authority and budgets capable of developing technology and higher education policy.[9] This goes far beyond anything that could be achieved in partnership with business by even the largest British local authorities—even before they had all responsibility for post-school education removed from them at the end of the 1980s.

We lightly use the term 'business community' without inquiring whether the cluster of businesses we have in mind form anything remotely resembling a community or are simply a number of isolated firms.

[8] W. Streeck, 'The Logics of Associative Action and the Territorial Organization of Interests: the case of German *Handwerk*', in Streeck, *Social Institutions and Economic Performance: Studies of Industrial Relations in Advanced Capitalist Economies*, Sage, London, 1992.

[9] J. Esser, 'Does Industrial Policy Matter?', in C. Crouch and D. Marquand, eds., *The New Centralism*, Blackwell, Oxford, 1989.

German businesses in most sectors inherit and then recreate the mutual obligations, inter-personal and inter-organisational links that make a community in the richer sense.[10] One does not necessarily have to approve of the things that German businesses do on the strength of these inter-firm ties to recognise here: (i) the scope for collective action they enjoy; (ii) the way in which this can extend beyond relations of pure contract and induce co-operative behaviour; (iii) the institutional roots of this; but (iv) its resemblance to the kind of behaviour that we commonly regard as moral or normative. Their mode of proceeding has the status of Hirsch's 'moral legacy'.

Skill formation

Perhaps the best example of how this structure of co-operative capitalism works is in the German model of vocational training and apprenticeship. The guild legacy predisposes to a high level of occupational skill in two different ways, both stemming from 'archaic tradition'. First, the organisational base of the *Kammer* provides the means for collective action necessary if firms competing in open markets are to be willing to invest in the creation of skill, to play their part in training apprentices even during recessions. German labour markets are open; they do not depend on workers staying all their lives with a particular company. Their skills are transferable and publicly certificated. The system works only because all companies are tied into it through organisational cohesion and sanctions.[11]

Secondly, the idea of the skilled craftsman is a direct legacy of the guild model. It might seem a piece of far-fetched Wagnerian romanticism to see any connection between a medieval Nürnberg shoemaker and a polyvalent skilled worker operating the console of a computerised production unit in a late 20th-century Siemens plant. But the connection is there and comes directly through the line of *Kammer* organisation. This lineage is seen most obviously in *Handwerk*; but the industrial concept of skill has developed by approximation to that ideal as embodied in the concept of apprenticeship as the central form of training. The *Meister*, the skilled master at his trade who combines the roles of foreman, practitioner and trainer of apprentices is as much a reality in an advanced giant factory as in a craft workshop. This is a good example of what is meant by the embodiment of values in institutions; the values of advanced manual skill and pride in that skill are embodied in the statutory and corporatist

[10] K. Dyson, 'Cultural Issues and the Single European Market', *The Political Quarterly*, 64, 1, January 1993.

[11] W. Streeck, 'Skills and the Limits of Neo-Liberalism: the Enterprise of the Future as a Place of Learning', *Work, Employment and Society*, 3, pp. 90–104, 1989; and *The Role of the Social Partners in Vocational Training and Further Training in the Federal Republic of Germany*, Berlin, CEDEFOP, 1987; D. Soskice, 'Reconciling Markets and Institutions: an Interpretation of the German Apprenticeship System', Wissenschaftszentrum, Berlin, unpublished manuscript, 1992.

87

mechanisms of the artisan sector and in the regulations governing occupational training in industry. They would not have survived merely as ideas.

The involvement of individual companies in apprenticeship prevents German training from being carried out by organisations beyond the reach of individual firms; companies and their rapidly changing technological and organisational needs are engaged day-by-day in the whole edifice. Meanwhile the national scope of the system makes it possible for firms to pay reduced apprenticeship wages without much fear that young people will prefer to take unskilled but fully paid jobs. Because the coverage of the apprenticeship system is so extensive, there are very few such jobs and they are concentrated in dead-end sectors. The majority of young people accept the trade-off between low wages in the short term and the acquisition of a useful skill in the longer run.

There is a price to be paid for the advantages of this. It is slow-moving: change can be achieved only gradually and with a good deal of consultation. Both young people (who accept low apprentice wages) and companies (which forego the ability to cut losses during recessions) have to accept a level of deferred gratification if the system is to achieve its essentially long-term goals. It has, however, shown that it can adapt in certain kinds of market, especially those requiring a frequent up-dating and improvement of traditional skills (as in machine tool production); but perhaps not so much in the pursuit of newer industries requiring less skill from production staff (as in semi-conductors).

The financial system

The *Kammer* and other elements of the associational structure of German business are part of a coherent wider picture that includes, not only the collective bargaining system, but also the distinctive system of relations between banks and companies that protects from hostile takeover bids and encourages long-term decisions.[12] Training, as well as research and development, requires an ability by management to take a long-term view of investment decisions, paying out less in short-term profits to investors than would otherwise be possible. Companies' stock-exchange quotations are therefore likely to be under-estimates of their value. Long-term investments of this kind also require long-term commitments to product markets, even through lean years. In the absence of institutional protection of the kind afforded by German company ownership law and practice, companies investing heavily in training and other commitments would be vulnerable to hostile asset-stripping takeovers.

The central characteristics of German financial institutions are well known. The logic of their implications is similar to those described elsewhere in this volume by Ron Dore in relation to Japan—as is the extreme contrast they form with the United Kingdom. Stock exchanges and their

---

[12] Y. S. Hu, *National Attitudes and the Financing of Industry*, PEP, London, 1975.

associated secondary markets are relatively poorly developed. Firms finance investment through long-term loans from banks, who in turn take seats on firms' supervisory boards. Banks become involved in the management of firms. There is therefore an enduring commitment between creditor and company. This facilitates long-term decision-making, though, of course, in exchange for a constraint; management has to reveal more of what it does to its bankers, and bankers lose the option of walking away from a company in difficulties. The system also provides for some protection of the identity of a company; it is not easily sold, bought or asset-stripped; hostile takeovers are rare. If a company is in difficulties, the various stakeholders (creditors, management, workers) find themselves, unless the situation were to spin out of control, in a position where they must improve to survive. The option of cutting loose is virtually closed to them. At the same time managers have less fear that shareholders will sell out, so they do not face a need to keep dividends high at the expense of training and R&D.

An implication of this kind of economy is that it places a premium on engineering as opposed to financial skill as the heart of management and what the company is about. In terms of Hirschman's famous choice between mechanisms of exit and voice,[13] it is overall clearly a system of voice. When there are difficulties, all incentives lead people to stay to resolve the problem, and there are mechanisms for the participants to exchange the information necessary for this task. Membership of a firm's supervisory board gives bank staff a detailed insight into its working methods and plans, not just the bottom line of its accounts.

From a British or US point of view this can seem very claustrophobic. Banks might interfere with managerial discretion; one cannot easily get shot of a problem company by selling it, destroying it or asset-stripping it. Commitment, by and to managers, owners and workers, is a central characteristic of institutions which bind different groups to one another; forcing them to find solutions to problems. These are not moral commitments as such—they are produced by incentives and sanctions—but they have an ethical quality in their encouragement of long-term decision-making and the preservation of identity. One consequence of this can be the generation of trust—not the naive trust that is akin to faith, but the trust that emerges from an exchange relationship where there is strong evidence that the contract partner will continue to play the game and to follow consistent rules.

The origins of the banking system's relations to industry date back to the need to industrialise Germany in the latter 19th century, when it was felt to be lagging behind England, France, the USA and some other countries. Encouragement of long-term investment has therefore been built into the system. Over the years this has been highly successful in establishing the

---

[13] A. O. Hirschman, *Exit, Voice and Loyalty*, Harvard University Press, Cambridge, Mass, 1970.

© The Political Quarterly Publishing Co. Ltd. 1993.

distinctive product specialisms of German industry in sophisticated capital goods, machine tools and other advanced products. These need long investment times and, often, close relations with customers, sub-contractors and suppliers. If these relations were to change in rapid response to changing prices, there would be little incentive to undertake the risks of becoming committed to the big investments needed. Note this is not the 'soft option' of the safe contract. If the contract is long term but efficiency urgent, then people will simply work to ensure that agreements are kept. Again the keyword is commitment.

The place of labour

One of the main achievements of the Bonn Republic has been the integra-tion of organised labour into German public and economic life.[14] This is not necessarily easy for a system of this kind. A slow-moving, value-based economy will be conservative rather than liberal. The rules characteristic of liberalism are those of exit, not voice; commitments to other actors in the system are on a casual 'take it or leave it' basis. As a result there are no great anxieties over recognising new actors. When it is easy to drop and discard, there is less need to worry about whom to take up. That is the great attraction of this model of society, seen most clearly in the USA. Germany is not like that. Once admission to the system is achieved, an interest becomes part of the web of mutual obligations that cannot easily be ended. Therefore, initial admission is more problematic.

There is a distinct sense of insiders and outsiders. Politically this has been used in sinister ways.In Bismarck's day there was a clear distinction between persons defined as friends and those defined as enemies of the regime (*Reichsfreunde* and *Reichsfeinde*). Under Hitler this kind of thinking acquired horrifying implications. The historic difficulties of organised labour's struggle for acceptance and recognition are part of this pattern. Within a system based on long-term commitments, the obverse of gains to insiders are losses to outsiders.

After the false start of Weimar, Labour's incorporation was eventually achieved following 1949 through characteristic German institutions. German collective bargaining is based on a complex web of relationships that binds together different levels of collective organisation on each side of industry, as well as between employers and unions. This prevents either side from cutting loose from obligations and thereby imposes on them a logic of long-term co-operation and co-ordination.

In the background are again the collective organisations of German business, in this case the employers' associations. These are highly representative and have certain coercive powers, based on their ability to finance disputes, and on the legal right that they share with trade unions by

[14] W. Streeck, *Social Institutions and Economic Performance: Studies of Industrial Relations in Advanced Capitalist Economies*, Sage, London, 1992, chs. 5 and 6.

which the partners to any collective agreement can have its terms imposed on the whole sector, irrespective of whether all the firms or workers in question are members. There is a careful meshing of industries and regions within this structure, so that levels of co-ordination build up gradually from local to national. The dominance of the giant metal industry (covering steel-making as well as the whole engineering industry) sets a tone that virtually guarantees a more-or-less even rate of increase across all industries and areas.

On the labour side, unions are similarly and reciprocally structured: capital and labour organise in each other's image. The metal industry union, IG Metall, the largest union in the world, is so centrally located within the economy that, although it is a relatively militant organisation, it has to accept responsibility for the likely consequences of its demands on German international trade. Alongside IG Chemie, the union representing workers in the chemical industry, the other heartland of the great German export machine, it imparts this sensitivity to the rest of the trade-union movement.

At plant and company level, this structure intertwines with the system of co-determination constituted by workers' representation on supervisory boards (along with banks and other interests) and, more important, the works councils or *Betriebsräte*. These latter are a non-union company-level system of representation equipped with certain statutory powers to protect workers' interests within the firm. While the unions often resent the need to work alongside a non-union form of representation, because they are forced to do so they have found ways of making themselves useful to works councillors, take care to keep in detailed contact with them and their concerns, and have often given them roles within the unions' own structures. This also imparts to the union a moderation and co-operative approach based on companies' market prospects, as *Betriebsräte* never want to run the risk of crippling the company for which they work. Meanwhile, the system also provides a base for workers' role in the company community.

Among the important rights of *Betriebsräte* are those concerning the protection of employment. It is very difficult (if not impossible) to make workers in a German firm redundant or put them on short time without the works council's agreement. Just as unions sometimes find the need to co-operate with *Betriebsräte* irksome, but in fact benefit from doing so, employers often find these constraints difficult. But the consequence is that they, too, work hard to co-operate to ensure that redundancies and short-time working are rarely needed; that there is an emphasis on retraining rather than dismissal; and that they communicate the nature of difficulties to the work force so that the works council might come to understand and accept them.

At times when organised labour's market or political power is strong, as in the late 1960s or early 1970s, German unions weighed down with their national economic responsibility, their internal centralisation and their

91

need to work with works councils seem clumsy poor relations alongside the fast-moving, flexible militancy of the British shop-steward movement; but at times of recession like the present the mutual commitments between them, employers and the law appear in a different light. German industrial relations, including the level of trade union membership, have remained remarkably stable throughout the 1980s and early 1990s. The labour story is very similar to the training story and the finance story; this is an economy rich in mutual commitments among heavily organised actors caught in a web of reciprocity. This prevents any major interest benefiting from opportunistic actions, but it also protects against suffering at the expense of someone else's opportunism. Germany might not have a strong Keynesianism, but if an essential point about Keynesianism is the smoothing of both extremes of the trade cycle, the German political economy has its own mechanisms for achieving that goal, and not just in the economic field.

The Bundesbank

By itself, this could all be a corporatist nightmare, a protectionist producers' cartel whereby old pals protect each other from adversity and from disruptive newcomers. It is prevented from becoming this by two forces. First is the *inclusionary* nature of the system itself, a fundamental (and, for Germany, original) achievement of the Federal Republic. Virtually the whole national economy is involved in this system; all it can conspire against is itself. There are few outsiders to the system on whom its undesired externalities can be dumped.

The second force is the Bundesbank which stands outside the network of corporatist relations: an inaccessible fact of life that has to be taken for granted and cannot be manipulated. The great co-operative and institutional edifice of the German economy exists alongside an institution that stands beyond its reach and imposes on it a tough monetary discipline. The German central bank is constitutionally autonomous and cannot be given instructions by the federal government; no-one can put pressure on it. The flexibility and strategic capacity of German corporatism, organised for doing deals and reaching agreements though it is, can never negotiate with the Bank's requirements. All policy, therefore, whether of public authorities, firms or unions, has to take account of its ultimate anti-inflationary constraint.

In an economy in which most social interests have to be incorporated, an attempt to do so through feather-bedding and failure to advance efficiency creates inflation. The strength of the Bundesbank's counter-inflationary stance closes off that beguiling but futile escape route. Without the discipline of this autonomous central bank, a system as ridden with inter-organisational links as the German one could well lapse into protectionist inefficiency, which may explain the strength of the commitment to maintain the bank's position. But, by the same token, without the

92

© The Political Quarterly Publishing Co. Ltd. 1993.

elaborate corporatism that enables groups of companies, or employers' associations and unions, to make long-term co-operative deals and to keep reproducing a skilled, well trained work force, that kind of monetarist dominance could well produce a permanently recessive economy with no growth priority.

This is the answer to the famous jibe of Adam Smith, that wherever tradespeople combine together they are likely to make a conspiracy against the public, a remark widely quoted by new-right economists in their critique of corporatist and institutionalised economies. There is a paradox about the German (also the Austrian, Dutch and Swiss) econo-mies: they combine exceptionally strong forms of corporatist co-ordination and co-operation among firms with a virtually neo-classical rigidity of central banking institutions. Which is the secret of success, which the drag on the system? The answer is that both are needed, each acting as a check against the potential excesses of the other.

Germany and Britain compared

Two conclusions can be drawn from this account of the character of the German economic system. First is the fact that it is an integrated system, an *ensemble*. The different components combine to produce its character-istic outcomes, and it would be difficult to alter some without changing or even damaging the operation of the whole. This point should not be over-stated. The system was not 'designed' as such, and it is quite probable that somewhat different configurations might work similarly. Also, one should not assume that it works in an unimprovably perfect way. It is vulnerable to criticism at a number of points. It is not easy to start entirely new industries. If organised labour never reaches the depths of weakness of, say, the French or US union movements, it also never has a chance to rival the power of the Scandinavian. Women and ethnic minorities rarely get the best deals from the great training system. In general, it remains difficult to enter—though predictions in the early 1980s that environmental issues would never penetrate the producers' cartels proved unfounded: ecological concerns have been taken far more seriously than in the ostensibly more openly pluralistic systems of the UK and the USA.

But the main reason for pointing to the *ensemble* character of this economy is to warn against institutional imitation that pulls out small non-detachable components, or components ripped from their historical logic.

The second conclusion is to grasp the quality of this kind of capitalism, that cannot be reduced to the logics of either market or state, or even to a mix of both, but to institutions as they have been defined here: arrange-ments of organisations which develop rules of conduct that transcend pure market contract, and which acquire something of the qualities of values. This makes possible the long-term and collective-goods nature of many of the decisions in the German economy. These in turn both make possible and benefit from the long-term treatment of the labour contract.

There is no space here to enter into a detailed comparison between this German model and the British one, but a few clear contrasts can usefully be indicated. However, it should be noted that historically British society has in no way been lacking in institutions in the sense discussed above. On the contrary, in the 19th and much of the 20th centuries German, like French, observers often admired that strength of British civil society that did not require constant state action to induce publicly-oriented behaviour. (The tradition of voluntary local justices of the peace was an institution that particularly excited attention.) Britain was the country that produced the original trade unions, friendly societies, charities as voluntary (as opposed to church) bodies.

We have also had a deeply-rooted sense of 'the public' meaning something other than 'the state', an area of publicly-oriented voluntary endeavour. The National Trust is a very good example. Reciprocally, it has consequently been possible for the British state to set up institutions in the same mould—public but independent of itself: the British Broadcasting Corporation (at least until current reforms), or the former University Grants Committee. It would therefore be inaccurate to regard the British tradition of a low-profile state as implying a pure market society. Instead, there was a rich tapestry of social institutions.

There has, however, long been a very strong core of British institutions which *are* pure market. This was, after all, the society in which the free market economy was invented. The British political legacy of the mid-20th century can now be seen to have had two components. On one side was the country's past as the first industrial nation, with a heavy inheritance of manufacturing industry that had become inflexible. With this had developed a pattern of compromise and give-and-take in industrial relations between employers and unions, combined with the generally decentralised, non-strategic pattern of organisation that both sides had produced. Also, the country had developed, after World War II, a strong welfare state. These features fitted well into the country's general record of expansive, benign institutions and a genial care for a public interest, conceived in a non-strategic way. The general character of this side of the British legacy was relaxed, even laid back, rather slow-moving and uncalculating—and, in the circumstances of the last three decades of the century, becoming increasingly vulnerable.

The alternative model also has its heart in the unforced character of the British industrial revolution, but not in its legacy of old manufacturing industry; rather in the idea of *laissez faire* capitalism. Markets should be unimpeded by institutions and should move smartly and flexibly. The acme of this side of British life was the City of London and its associated financial sector. A set of markets geared to very rapid decisions and short-term calculations. This model informed British company law, with its emphasis on share-holding, short-term bank-lending and dividend calculations, where the hostile takeover was an accepted part of business life and prevented managers from undertaking long-term investments that might push the real assets of a company above its quoted value. There was a further hostility, or at least indifference, to industrial interests in the role of the pound sterling and its over-valuation, and in the City's international orientation.

In our finance-based economy companies' primary means of raising new investment is through the issue of new stocks or bonds.[15] These are purchased by numerous individuals and institutions, each free to buy and sell them at will. As a result, relations between owners and their companies tend to be distant, or 'arm's length'. Unlike the German system of banks' representation on supervisory boards, this form of financial market is subject to imperfect flows of information or what economists describe as 'insider-outsider' problems. Shareholders, for example, see a fall in earnings and are unable to determine whether this signals the start of a decline in performance or is the result of long-term investments that have reduced short-term profitability. Managers, for their part, will be reluctant to release information that will adversely affect the value of their stock. In this institutional situation, financial experts will tend to discount company pronouncements regarding future performance, focusing their research on those factors that can be most easily forecast, or what game theory dubs 'focal points'. In this case, fluctuations in current levels of profitability or return on investment. As a consequence, investors will tend to display little loyalty to a given corporation, being concerned more with what the share price will be in three days rather than three years. Once again: low trust; short time horizons.

Things are made worse by the fact that our regulatory system deliberately places few restrictions on hostile takeovers.[16] Managers who make long-term investments that depress profits—such as training and research and development—face the risk of an outside interest seizing control over the company and raising the share price by slashing investment or selling off the assets of corporation that are undervalued by the market. Even if management is successful in fighting off a takeover bid, it may leave the company so saddled with debt that it cannot afford long-term investments. More generally, managements of companies in capital markets of this kind are constantly aware of the risks involved and will themselves try to deter potential asset-stripping takeovers by keeping their investments in R&D and training low. When this practice is widespread across an economy, such investment will be permanently and almost universally sub-optimal. Even in cases where managers are not directly responsible to shareholders,

---

[15] Much of this discussion draws on D. Finegold, 'The Low-Skill Equilibrium: an Institutional Analysis of Britain's Education and Training Failure', University of Oxford, unpublished D.Phil thesis, 1992, ch. III.

[16] M. Jensen, 'Eclipse of the Public Corporation', *Harvard Business Review*, 68, 5, pp. 61–74, 1989.

95

their investment timescales may be influenced by the financial market and the criteria for evaluating performance which it sets.[17]

Very large corporations may be able to finance a significant proportion of investment through retained earnings and have in the past been less vulnerable to hostile takeovers because of the high cost of acquiring them. However, the advent of new financing mechanisms during the deregulation wave of the 1980s has eased this constraint. Through such a device as the leverage buy-out, under which a potential purchaser can call on long and extensive potential credit lines to finance a major purchase, corporate raiders, like the currency speculators, now have an easier task.

This second face of Britain was clearly at loggerheads with the first, but for many years the two co-existed. This was possible because both models shared a lack of interest in long-term strategy: the former because it had no capacity for it, the second because it was geared to the very short term. This coincidence of interest was expressed in the particular form of British Keynesianism. The Treasury manipulated a few central policy instruments to sustain demand and therefore employment (favouring the interests associated with the first Britain), but having done that, left the economy alone to be run by virtually free market forces (the second Britain). Keynesianism by itself was a short-termist policy. Keynes's famous remark 'In the long run we're all dead' was directed against free-market economists who advocated leaving the inter-war recession alone until in the long run it righted itself; but it also gives away the short-term fixation of his own ideas and their essential compatibility with the second model.

As the manufacturing sector visibly deteriorated from at least the 1960s on, governments tried various interventions, but none that succeeded in reconciling the gap between the two Britains. An attempt at indicative planning by the Labour governments of 1964 and 1966 was undermined by a postponement of a devaluation of the pound sterling that was at least partly in deference to the City's need for an exceptionally strong and stable home currency.

The signal achievement of the Thatcher governments after 1979 was to break the log-jam of the stand-off consensus between the two Britains by siding unequivocally with the second: the Britain of short-term financial calculation against that of a declining manufacturing base. The attack on the public service and on a whole set of other institutions flowed from that; to make the choice of model unambiguous Britain had to be forced out of commitments that contradicted the short-term market model. Public expenditure that both detracted from market forces and, in some of its forms, imposed expensive costs of infrastructural investments, had to go. Other institutions that did not follow the rules of the short-term market either had to reform themselves in the desired direction or decline.

By the early 1990s the victory was virtually complete. Because of the

[17] K. Williams, J. Williams and D. Thomas, *Why Are the British Bad at Manufacturing?*, Routledge and Kegan Paul, London, 1989.

sectoral and regional composition of the Conservative electorate (employed primarily in the private services sector and living in southern England), the collapse of northern manufacturing and the public services could be managed with equanimity—though the decline of the environment of southern England that has resulted from the major shift of population towards it remains a potential major vulnerability.

There is now, however, a new problem: can an economy based so thoroughly on the services sector pay its way in the world? For a period a confident and novel answer was given to this: it was no longer necessary to do so. Conservative spokesmen began to argue that, provided government maintained a tight rein on public spending and on inflation, overseas investors would be willing to hold stocks of the currency and would thereby finance the deficit on the trading account. They hoped to be able to produce an economy that, based on the flexibility of a workforce decreasingly supported by trade unions, protective legislation and employment security, combined with rapid short-term adjustments by the financial sector, would be as strong as the German economy but by using entirely different means. The Germans might have a mighty industrial economy based on advanced technology and a skilled work force, defenders of British policy would argue, but they were forced to move slowly and expensively, partly because of the nature of long-term technological investment and partly because their consensual way of doing things prevented them from imposing hard decisions on the workforce without consultation or agreement. Lean-limbed, fast-moving, post-Thatcher Britain would soon be able to look the mighty overweight Germany in the eye.

The ignominious retreat of sterling from the European Exchange Rate Mechanism in October 1992 ended that vision. Because of the ambition of rivalling the Deutsche Mark, sterling had entered the ERM at an unsustainable rate in the first place, and eventually this truth was demonstrated. As the recession deepened, matters went out of control again, and many of the flexible firms in southern England that had mushroomed during the late 1980s boom collapsed. The lean-limbed service sector companies often proved to be as easy go as easy come. It is an inbuilt characteristic of the 'exit' model and contrasts with the slowness of movement in both directions under the German 'voice' model.

It is a significant irony that in the UK the financial sector alone not only retained a full range of institutional support throughout the Thatcher/ Major period, but had it enhanced in an example of pure corporatist policy-making. Despite its status as a set of the purest possible markets, the City had long had, not only its sense of history, its constitutionally distinct geographical area, its cultural symbols, but a set of regulatory mechanisms and institutions, both formal and informal. In 1987 much of the existing regulatory structure was abolished, and a new era of deregulation markets established. However, the deregulated markets were subject to a new supervisory regime, as the government established a Securities

97

Exchange Commission to oversee the firms engaged in the restructured securities market. This agency is elected by members of the City, and is therefore an example of self-regulation, but it was set up by government and exercises a statutory power; firms are compulsorily subject to its authority. Ironically, this is the nearest thing in Britain to a German *Kammer*—though the guild links which are also part of the City's heritage long ago became, in contrast to the German case, entirely ceremonial and in no way relate to modern industrial skills and apprenticeships. The ironic twist is that these mechanisms that impart an institutional privilege to the financial sector ensure its short-termist *modi operandi* are imposed on the manufacturing sector, forcing it to become deinstitutionalised and fragile.

Hirsch, writing in the mid-1970s, saw the moral legacy of modern capitalist societies as a 'depleting' one. In the case of Britain that depletion has been deliberately accelerated in the years after he wrote. Adam Smith's present-day admirers do not share his views about non-market legacies, and regard all procedures that do not have the attributes of short-term calculative exchange as sources of allocative inefficiency.

If Hirsch is right, these legacies are bound to deteriorate over time, assisted or not. However, until now the German case has resisted this interpretation. Even the brief outline given above has indicated some ways in which archaic, essentially pre-capitalist mechanisms have been capable of renewal, recreation and reinterpretation. A detailed study of the historical development of the *Meister*, the *Kammer*, or *Handwerk* would all demonstrate this. If the institutions can be remodelled in the light of and exposed to modern competitive pressures, they can reinforce the values they embody. It is only values that are left stranded, not incorporated institutionally, that will wither on the historical shore.

That at least has been the lesson of recent German history, especially striking given the upheavals and hiatus of the 1918 to 1949 period. There is now an opportunity to observe these institutions under a new pressure. The country is unifying the *Länder* of the successful Bonn Republic with eastern territories that passed from the *Hitlerzeit* to four decades of Communist rule. At the same time, Japan and several newly-industrialised countries of the Pacific rim are beginning to extend successful industrial production into sectors where in the past the German skilled labour system reigned supreme. How well will German industry respond to this challenge? In particular, will characteristic co-operative institutions develop in the eastern *Länder*; while in the other former Communist countries around them Anglo-American short-term, pure-exchange methods are being imposed by international creditors as the one best way of creating a successful capitalism?

HUMAN RESOURCES AND HUMAN INGENUITY

JUDITH MARQUAND*

In *Capitalisme contre Capitalisme*, Albert[1] distinguishes what he regards as the conflictual Anglo-American model of capitalism from the consensual 'Rhenish' model. Attitudes towards what the Anglo-American tradition terms 'human resources' appear to lie near the core of his distinction between the models. Yet, in a world allegedly dominated by multinationals who in large part make their own choice about the conduct of their own affairs, the continuation of a strong distinction is perhaps puzzling. Where does the truth lie? Where within it is Britain to be found?

An anecdote illustrates that a distinction of some kind does indeed need to be drawn. During a recent group visit to Germany, British industrialists and others with active involvement in the British training system saw the involvement of German firms in training in their local communities. One leading industrialist asked his German employer hosts 'why are German employers so involved in training?'. The Germans looked puzzled. After a time the reply came back: 'we don't understand your question.' My subject is the nature of that mutual misunderstanding.

I start by asking why the way in which the two systems feature human resources and human ingenuity is so central to the theoretical distinction between different styles of capitalism. I then look at Albert's very definite views. Are they correct? Do they go to the heart of the matter? Thirdly, I look at what is actually happening in the United States, Britain and Germany. I focus particularly on Britain, because I argue that it represents a rather interesting intermediate position. In particular, I distinguish between what firms choose to do on the one hand, and the formal training systems and the nature of public policy on the other. Finally, I draw conclusions about the fundamental distinctions which different human resource development and management systems do seem to illuminate.

Theory: the centrality of human resources and human ingenuity

We can start from received Anglo-American economic theory. One of its many paradoxes is that a theory which purports to describe the way in which optimal decisions are made about the production and allocation of

* The author is director of the Centre for Training Policy Research, University of Sheffield and was formerly Head of Evaluation and Research at the Government's Training Agency.

[1] Michel Albert, *Capitalisme contre Capitalisme*, Editions du Seuil, Paris, 1991.

goods and services has no logical space for an understanding of how decisions about new goods and services (or indeed changed goods and services) come about.

The introduction of new goods and services is to some extent unforeseeable, and their consequences much more so. The theorists do admit that uncertainty is pervasive, but their response is only to argue that we should insure against foreseeable risks. Thus they push the unknown, the consequences of creativity, to the boundaries of human thought and action. The theorists treat such activities as though they were rather awkward ones on the periphery of society. Is it too fanciful to think that this goes with the marginalisation of the artist, the inventor, the sick, the delinquent and the mad?

To put it more formally, Witt[2] explains that, in the orthodox position:

> Optimal choice of actions can only be based on perceived or expected consequences. In the case of unknowable future outcomes, expectations cannot be formed and, hence, cannot motivate action, unless it is assumed that people systematically err with regard to the unknowability condition or deliberately ignore it.

But novelty is crucial to human activity, even to economic activity—and imagination is essential to the creation of all novelty. All decision-makers' *perception* of choices is influenced by their imagination—their capacity to envisage and so to create novelty. But 'imagination' and the 'capacity to create novelty' are not God-given. They can be fostered. It is here that the link lies between innovation and training. This link requires further demonstration.

Let us define training as 'deliberate intervention to foster learning—the development of *knowledge, skills and understanding*—which is relevant to economic activity'.

Now, for the individual who learns, all application of learning is a form of innovative activity. All perception of the relevance of something which we already know to the analysis of a new set of circumstances and its application to their mastery is innovation.

In terms of the difference which this makes to individual behaviour and of the new competences which this difference indicates, then the individual or the firm which undertakes activities which are new to it—although they may be well-known to others—is as much an innovator as is the path-breaker at the frontiers of human endeavour.

People can learn, and it follows from the link between learning and innovation that they can learn to innovate. Moreover, you need an institutional structure which can foster innovation, if an economy is to change and grow. Heavily rule-bound societies tend to be innovation averse. Thus, to quote Witt[3] again,

---

[2] Ulrich Witt, 'Reflections on the Present State of Evolutionary Economic Theory' in G. Hodgson and E. Screpanti, eds., *Rethinking Economics*, Edward Elgar, Aldershot, 1991, p. 88.

[3] *Ibid.*, p. 96.

a transition has to be made from primitive, innovation-averse institutions which threaten and punish all attempts to innovate to institutions which approve or encourage innovativeness.

Here, then, we have a paradox. Why is the allegedly open, democratic American society and economy apparently so much less innovative, so much less successful in developing and using human ingenuity for economic and social purposes than the allegedly rule-bound, rigid German one?

On the one hand, the American and British rhetoric claims that short-term flexibility and profit maximisation are all-important. Do firms in America and Britain really behave like this?

Germans on the other hand complain all the time about rigidities of their labour market. Yet this inflexible labour market—if it really is so—appears to go hand in hand with a very efficient economy. The very efficient economy does indeed produce some of the alleged benefits of the ideal type of an Anglo-American free market. So what is really happening?

I have argued that the development and use of human ingenuity is central to economic success. One directly relevant aspect of such development and use of human ingenuity is the strategy adopted for training itself and the associated institutionally-embedded area of human resource management. It follows that the way in which these different societies handle training and the consequences of training—trained people—in the work context is likely to throw light on the economic and social consequences of their different forms of capitalism.

Albert's position

Albert makes some very definite statements about training and related management questions within the firm. He argues that co-partnership is of major importance in the Rhenish model and also that five dimensions of training activity and outcomes are significant:

— there are higher proportions of people with qualifications in Germany than in France or Britain;
— there is a more egalitarian system of training in Germany than in the US or France (and he might also have added, Britain), with more emphasis on intermediate skills;
— training in Germany is largely paid for by employers and by federal subsidies. Emphasis is placed on acquiring appropriate work behaviour: precision, punctuality, reliability;
— professionalism is recognised; promotion is on the basis of proved performance;
— there are close links between firms and universities: the former support almost all the teaching at the latter.

101

Now these facts are broadly correct, and indeed it may be appropriate to place emphasis on the contrast between Germany and France in these respects, as Albert does. But comparison with American and Britain is rather more complex. Albert has packed five different propositions into what he presents as one statement of the significant differences between the systems. The five propositions need to be unpicked. Why has he selected these aspects?

Albert[4] presents the theoretical structure of his two models:

> According to the Anglo-Saxon model, if you are to maximise competitiveness of a firm, you have to maximise competitiveness of those whom it employs. Thus you must, always and everywhere, recruit the best and pay them their market value at all times, or else you will lose them. Pay is essentially individual and precarious, like employment itself.

In other words, Albert's Anglo-American model is the short-term profit maximising model of the neo-classical economists.

On the other hand:

> for the Rhenish-Japanese model, this is not the essential point. Firms do not have the right to treat their employees simply as factors of production which are bought and sold in the market place like raw materials. Instead, the firm has a certain duty of security, of trust, of training, which is expensive. Thus, rather than pay everyone his immediate market value, the firm must plan career structures, smooth curves, avoid destructive rivalries.

And my earlier argument makes the link (which I think Albert does not) between such institutional structures, combined with an emphasis on training, learning and hence the capacity to innovate in all kinds of ways, and the consequent successful economic performance.

This, then, is Albert's statement of the theory of the Rhenish-Japanese model, but we need to ask what actually happens:

— does this contrast really hold?
— how in a world of multi-nationals and international managers can much contrast remain?
— how does the German system *really* differ from the US and UK ones?
— do the differences have the consequences which Albert ascribes to them?

For Albert's account of the theory of the Rhenish system sounds very like the theory of the American-inspired school of human resource management.

What actually happens: firms

I distinguish between two major dimensions: on the one hand what firms choose to do, and on the other public policy and formal training systems. I

---

[4] *Op. cit.*, p. 137 (my translation).

shall argue that Britain is trying to use public policy to move training behaviour in the German direction, despite much of the recent rhetoric, whilst its underlying position is nearer to the American one.

Let us start by looking at what firms are actually doing. First, the funding of training. The British Government's funding study, *Training in Britain*[5] uses 1986/7 data and shows that in Britain in that year total expenditure on training was about 8 per cent of gross domestic product. We do not have adequate international comparisons yet, although work at the European Commission should make these possible fairly soon. But the 8 per cent of GDP on training compares reasonably well with the 5 per cent of GDP which was the 1987 public expenditure on health care, or the 4 per cent which was the public expenditure on education. This is not the expenditure of a country which does not train. Why then are the results so poor?

There are several possible reasons. First, there is the historical legacy. There was very little training in Britain in the past; what we have today is a recent substantial increase. We still have the backlog of millions of poorly-trained people in the labour force. This is certainly part of the answer.

Secondly, it is possible that much training is or has been of poor *quality*. There is an element of truth in this, too, but it has to be taken together with another part of the legacy: the need to use training to make up for deficiencies in the British education system. How much of what counts as training in Britain would have been learnt at school elsewhere, or learnt more efficiency elsewhere because of what had already been learnt at school? This is part of the answer too.

Of the £33 billion spent on training in 1986–7, £18 billion was spent by employers (and £11 billion of this private sector employers). £8 billion was spent by individuals, mainly in the form of earnings foregone. £7 billion was spent by Government. Even though the figures are subject to a considerable margin of error—especially for the employers[6]—this does appear to be a system where employers and Government pay for the bulk—about three quarters—of the training which takes place. In this respect the British system appears to be very much as Albert alleges that the German one is.

If we look more closely at employers' expenditure on training,[7] we see that nearly half (48 per cent) of employees received some training of some sort in 1986/7. Very large firms spent more than others and very small firms spent slightly less. Training was concentrated heavily on initial training, both of apprentices and of other new recruits. More training was

[5] Training Agency, *Training in Britain. A Study of Funding, Activity and Attitudes. Main report*, HMSO, London, 1989.

[6] Paul Ryan, 'How much do Employers spend on Training? An Assessment of the *Training in Britain* Estimates', in *Human Resource Management Journal*, vol. 1, No. 4, 1991, pp. 55–76.

[7] Training Agency, *Training in Britain. A Study of Funding Activity and Attitudes. Employers' Perspectives*, HMSO, London, 1989.

103

received by men than by women, especially in the older age group. The main difference, however, was that firms with more than the average amount of training did consistently better on a whole range of indicators of performance than firms with rather little. A high level of training was associated with higher than average levels of a whole range of human resource development and management processes: formal staff appraisal, a policy of career moves, formal communication channels, opportunities for general education, a policy of secondment or exchanges and counselling on careers or personal matters.

Moreover, there has been a big rise in the training of those in employment since 1984. There has been a 70 per cent increase in the Labour Force Survey figures of those who received training in the month before the questionnaire. It now stands at about 14 per cent. But we need the figures which the European Commission will produce in 1994 before we can make much *comparative* sense of this.

What the figures do show is that even Britain is a country where many firms train and where some appear to view training as part of a wider human resource management policy. But many firms, it seems, still do not. Many of them do not really know what they spend their training resources on and many of them do not seem to *think* much about training at all.

The personnel function

To start to get behind this, we need to look at the major debate which has been going on in the industrial relations and personnel scene in Britain in the past few years about the role of the personnel function. Purcell,[8] for example, has been asking whether there is a role for central personnel departments in the increasingly decentralised major companies of the 1980s and 1990s, where management responsibilities are pushed increasingly down the line. The answers so far are ambiguous. The ambiguity relates to questions of company style, which in turn seem to relate to questions of the human resource management style which the company adopts.

It could be argued that only where human resource management is taken seriously (and this happens only where strategic planning is taken seriously), will training and career structure—long-term thinking about individuals—assume the central role that its relevance to innovative behaviour suggests should be assigned to it.

We can start with a definition of strategic planning taken from Goold and Campbell.[9] In essence they contrast the 'strategic planners' who seek

[8] John Purcell, 'The impact of corporate strategy on human resource management' in John Storey, ed., *New Perspectives in Human Resource Management*, Routledge, London, 1989, pp. 67–91.

[9] M. Goold and A. Campbell, *Strategies and Styles: The Role of the Centre in Managing Diversified Corporations*, Blackwell, Oxford, 1987.

long-term competitive advantage through collaborative means, with the 'strategic controllers' who also seek long-term competitive advantage but through much tighter central control and through emphasis on perform-ance by the individual, and with the financial control companies—Albert's Anglo-American model—who emphasise short-term results.

Goold and Campbell look at sixteen major British companies. These include six which turn out to be flexible and strategic: strategic planners. Five of their sample turn out to be strategic controllers and five—BTR, Ferranti, GEC, Hanson Trust, and Tarmac—follow Albert's tight financial control model. They point out that, by contrast, Japanese firms are usually held up as models of 'strategic planning'. They then look at IBM, General Electric, Hewlett Packard and Matsushita to see whether their categories can be applied more widely. They find that they can and that the first three of these firms are strategic in their approach, although Matsushita does opt for a form of financial control model.

This tells us, then, that not all major British firms conform to Albert's Anglo-American model. Nor, it seems, do all major American ones.

Indeed, and here the argument moves more directly towards training, the whole human resource management model is imported from Amreica. If you read exhortatory texts like Peters and Waterman's *In Search of Excellence*[10] or Rosabeth Moss Kanter's *The Change Masters*,[11] you find that they urge a strategic planning style with a strong emphasis on develop-ing human resources, on developing people as assets.

Definitions of human resource management

What, then, do we mean by this 'human resource management'? Storey[12] gives possible meanings. The weakest is virtually a synonym for personnel management. The second is personnel management with selection, appraisal, reward and development approached in an integrated way. The third views employees as *resources*. This is a more business-oriented and integrated approach, which seeks added value through the sophisticated use of labour. The fourth approach seeks not only the integration of personnel management with business strategy, but also seeks to achieve *employee commitment*. Thus for Storey, human resource management focuses primarily on the individual in the firm rather than using collective negotiation. If Albert is correct, this is what we should expect of an approach which originates in the US. But human resource management is also compatible with a negotiated approach. It is compatible with reward structures for groups rather than individuals. The determining factor which allows a firm's personnel policy to be regarded as a strong version of

[10] Tom Peters and R. H. Waterman, *In Search of Excellence*, Harper and Row, New York, 1982.
[11] Rosabeth Moss Kanter, *The Change Masters*, Unwin, London, 1984.
[12] John Storey, *Developments in the Management of Human Resources*, Blackwell, Oxford, 1992.

human resource management policy is its integration with the firm's strategic planning and with development of career plans for individuals. Thus, where you have human resource management, you do not find Albert's Anglo-American model.

Moreover, it is clear that strategic approaches to human resources do not fit well with 'financial control' approaches to companies and that many British and indeed American firms are not of this 'financial control' kind. How far has human resource management progressed with them, and thus how far has a strategic approach to training progressed? Here we go behind the official Funding Study's statistics to look at processes; here again we can draw on Storey.

His picture is not an encouraging one. He looks at fifteen mainstream British companies and looks at the process of managing change away from the old style industrial relations system towards the newer human resource management system. All his companies had indeed started to move down this path by 1986–8, but they had almost all started with, or were moving towards, one particular version: unilateral top down imposition of a total package. There were only two exceptions to this: Ford with a total package of negotiated changes, and Plessey with some negotiated discrete initiatives.

How far were the companies in his sample succeeding? The difficulties did not appear to lie in opposition to the changes, but in the nature of the changes themselves. Even where there was a total package, it was usually not an integrated one. It was not thought through. There was not a structured approach. The integration of *training* with business planning, our particular concern here, is no exception.

Now training may be built in as a key concern in strategic planning companies which have strong central planning. But decentralisation to operational level is a major trend, and training may also be a key concern in such companies too. Here you can have diverse training policies in the different units of the same company. So the *diffusion* of changed attitudes and changed policies, even within the firm, becomes crucial if you want to integrate training with strategic planning. The Funding Study figures suggest that this integration had scarcely started in 1987. But it is worth noting that of Storey's fifteen case studies, six companies were 'learning companies' with a heavy emphasis on training (Peugeot Talbot, Jaguar, Bradford Metropolitan Council, Lucas, Rolls Royce and Whitbread). Eight more of the sample did place some emphasis on training within their human resource management initiatives, and only one ignored this dimension altogether. (With the publication of the Employers Manpower Skills Practice Survey fairly soon, we shall be able to bring the story up to 1991.)

Thus in big companies in Britain there appear to be many which adopt a strategic approach to human resources, an approach imported largely from America. There appear to be many which are adopting training initiatives more or less integrated with their strategy. The picture is still

106

very patchy, but it does not fit Albert's view of the United States and the United Kingdom. In the United Kingdom, it fits instead with the ancient pattern of unstructured muddle through. Moreover, the case studies suggest that the systematic training is often concentrated on managers: the traditional British neglect of the potential of all but the elite.

The continuing decentralisation of managerial responsibility places a heavier burden than before on wider networks to help bring about change. This leads to the other major theme of this paper.

Developments in public policy and the institutional framework

We have seen some remarkable developments in public policy towards training in Britain in the last half dozen years. I shall argue that, behind a smokescreen of rhetoric alleging that the new policies were borrowed from the United States, Britain has in fact been moving fast towards a 'Rhenish' system.

In the mid 1980s, Britain did not have explicit work-based standards, with qualifications to match them. Britain did not have machinery to co-ordinate training policy in the local labour market. Britain did not have close links between industry and education, either locally or sectorally. Yet in the early 1990s, the framework for all of these is in place. The crucial question today is 'can we make the new system work?'.

The new qualifications structure, the system of NVQs set up by the National Council for Vocational Qualification, is being dragged by the European Community policies towards compatibility with qualifications in other European countries. The questions which we have to ask are whether the NVQs will be adopted by the firms and individuals for whom they are designed. Will they be flexible enough? Will they be broad enough? The new National Education and Training Targets are being used to apply substantial leverage to the Training and Enterprise Councils to try to make them ensure that rapid progress is made towards adopting NVQs. The transitional problems are immense; the problem is not merely that of assimilation of old qualifications to the new system, but of the need to accredit prior learning. The need is also to persuade industry that NVQs are worthwhile. Both those firms who already have their own training systems and whose training is already to a very high standard, and those firms which do not believe in training to any significant extent at all have to be persuaded that NVQs are relevant to the way they conduct their business.

Whatever the problems, we do undoubtedly have a much more transparent system of qualifications than before. Moreover, there is industry involvement, through the lead bodies, in the design of standards. They are certainly not developed by training providers in isolation from industry.

In all of the development of the new system of standards and qualifications, the position is quite unlike that in the United States, which observes

107

© The Political Quarterly Publishing Co. Ltd. 1993.

the British changes with interest. It is possible that the industry involvement in developing the system is at least as great as in Germany. The Government attempts to involve British industry so closely in order to relate the qualifications (which match the standards) to what industry thinks it needs, to ensure relevance and so to make it easier for the new system to be embedded.

Training and Enterprise Councils

The machinery for developing and catalysing training policies in local labour markets is the Training and Enterprise Councils. These work closely with other major actors in their area, such as Local Education Authorities and Chambers of Commerce. They have problems. They are under-resourced, making do in large part with staff inherited from the old Training Agency Area Offices. They are under-funded. Most of their funding from the Government is given for them to spend on Youth Training and Employment Training, although they have a whole bunch of objectives from the Secretary of State which give them the very much wider remit of developing the training infrastructure and changing the attitudes of employers and individuals in their areas. Not only are they under-funded, but they have no support from legislation such as that which the German Chambers of Commerce enjoy. They have to operate by influence of various kinds. This at least means that they have to pay very close attention to partnership with other actors in their communities; they depend largely on goodwill and their own competence. Their task is a difficult one, but at least they are there, with a wide remit and a certain amount of money.

Not only do the TECs and the standard-setting process involve important employers directly, but many TECs place great emphasis on wider business/education partnerships and on membership schemes for firms. Colleges of Further Education are increasingly obliged to negotiate for custom directly with industry. The General National Vocational Qualifications (GNVQs), still newer than NVQs, attempt directly to bridge the academic/vocational divide. Direct involvement in training policies and their implementation is spreading far more widely through the community than before.

But there are the usual British problems of unplanned, unstructured, unresourced muddle through. The TECs themselves have to make plans, but Government does not appear to be prepared to make adequate plans or provision for the TEC system. Both Government and the TECs themselves are producing confused signals about where there should be co-operation and where there should be competition. There is a lack of clear public accountability—although TECs do have to produce Annual Reports and hold annual meetings. However, the TECs ensure that in local labour markets there is not an Anglo-American system such as Albert alleges.

Thus the recent British developments represent an attempt to move in the direction of the German system. There is an implicit acknowledgement of the strengths of the German local collaborative model.There is the development of an explicit qualification structure which allows the individual to follow a career path, more independent of any one employer than before. Within those qualifications which are newly developed, rather than those which are simply the adoption of old ones with a minor revision, personal and team skills are emphasised more than before.

Moreover, the German system is less rigid in some respects than it is often made out to be. There is indeed great rigidity in respect of the content of particular qualifications and in regard to qualification *levels* and the posts to which these entitle you. However, in the labour market itself there is not much rigidity in the range of jobs which a given qualification level enables you to hold. A very substantial proportion of young Germans work, once their apprenticeships are completed, in occupations other than those for which they were trained. (This indeed can be taken to demonstrate the importance of the generic elements in the skills which they acquire.)

Note that, by contrast, the American system does not have any of these formal structures. Diffusion and leverage become much harder to achieve. They have many exciting experiments, but enormous unevenness of standards. Indeed, the Americans are looking with interest at the British development of NVQs. Should they try to copy it?

Conclusions

I have argued that the effective development of human ingenuity and the ability to make good use of human resources are central to any developing, changing, economically successful economy. Albert alleges that the co-operative Rhenish system is superior to the competitive Anglo-American one in achieving this. But his argument is not as self-evident as it may appear, given four factors. First, there is the importance in all industrialised economies of multi-nationals. Secondly, there is the importance of international developments in management styles, much of it originating from the American approach to human resource management. Thirdly, the Germans are worried about the rigidities of their system. Fourthly, British public policy in recent years has been moving quickly in the direction of a German-style training system.

Whatever may be happening in the United States, what seems to be happening in Britain is that firms are training their workers to an increasing extent. There is growing transparency and portability of qualifications. There is unprecedented development of local training policy co-ordination, and there are improved industry links with education and training. All these are, however, at risk, not so much because of excessive competitiveness, but because of incompetence, muddle-through and inadequate resourcing.

A significant part of the blame for this in Britain must lie with the Anglo-American rhetoric. British firms have no concepts with wide currency which they can use to replace the stranglehold which the neo-classical economists seem to have. More influential still is the related dependency on accounting conventions which emphasise the short term. Managers and even accountants are starting to contrast the pro-active business approach, which entails a certain amount of risk-taking, with the risk-avoiding reactive accountancy conventions.[13]

People from or close to industry frequently tell me that what industry needs to know is 'why training pays', so that industry can embrace it more enthusiastically. I think many of those who make this point hope that a 'training culture' can simply be grafted on to existing practice. What I fear is that the answer has to be found by unpicking much deeper cultural traits. In Britain it is necessary to overcome the inability to structure thought and action. It is necessary to overcome the unwillingness to make use of the capacities of all and to engage openly in discussion with them. It is necessary to combat disbelief in the merits of collective organisation.

America shares some of these cultural traits, but by no means all of them.

Thus there is no simple Anglo-American model to contrast with the Rhenish one. Too many people believe in the rhetoric of the Anglo-American model for it to be easy to devise a convincing alternative and diffuse it. But one area where a start has in fact been made, in action more than in words, is the training system.

---

[13] See, for example, Anthony Hopwood, Michael Page and Stuart Turley, *Understanding Accounting in a Changing Environment*, Prentice Hall in association with the Institute of Chartered Accountants, Hemel Hempstead, 1990, pp. 62–4.

TRADE UNIONS AND NEW MANAGEMENT TECHNIQUES

DAVID NORMAN*

IN Britain today there are undoubtedly those, both industrialists and politicians, who would argue that trade unionism is in terminal decline, mortally wounded, it is said, by a fundamental shift away from collectivism in every sphere of national life, re-inforced and accelerated in Britain by the creation of a legal framework generally designed to make existence more difficult for the unions.

Furthermore, it is argued, trade unions are being made obsolete by a range of increasingly sophisticated management techniques, aimed at elevating the status of the individual in the workplace. A growing emphasis on the philosophy of personal advancement at work and a corresponding decline in the commitment to collective action through trade unions now hastens the slide into their eventual extinction. The experience of the United States, where less than one worker in five is a trade union member, is held up as the inevitable path which Britain will follow, ushering in an era of industrial harmony and co-operation.

There is no doubt that trade union membership has fallen and continues to fall in Britain, and a number of factors are clearly and readily identifiable as accounting for this phenomenon; but there is scant evidence to suggest that any significant proportion of that decline can genuinely be attributed to new and more subtle managerial techniques designed to motivate and (some might say) manipulate their workforce. In fact, from the practitioner's point of view, be they trade union official or, that equally endangered species, a personnel manager, the so called 'new management techniques' most notably as 'Human Resource Management' (HRM) , which have been embraced with such gusto in recent times by British employers, are neither particularly *new* in their approach nor *revolutionary* in their impact on what the conservatives amongst us still refer to, no doubt anachronistically, as the 'shop floor'. A review of the evidence leads to the conclusion that other more basic forces are at work in causing union contraction. Whilst the British trade union movement unquestionably has to cope with many real problems, the erosion of its power and authority by managerial techniques such as HRM does not figure large.

In Britain, as in most western countries, trade unionism has been in retreat for more than a decade. Between 1981 and 1991 affiliated

---

* The author is General Treasurer (Senior National Officer) of the National Communications Union and a former Research Officer with the Post Office Engineering Union. He previously worked as a Research Assistant with the National Board for Prices & Incomes, and for the Commission on Industrial Relations and Office of Manpower Economics.

membership of the Trades Union Congress (TUC) (which embraces all but a handful of British trade unions) fell from more than 12 million to a little more than 7 million. Trade union members as a percentage of the workforce fell during the same period from a fraction under 50 per cent to a little over 37 per cent.[1]

A number of factors have undoubtedly played their part in this rapid decline. Principle among these is what one informed observer of the industrial relations scene has referred to in fashionably environmental terms as the 'erosion of their natural habitat'. That is to say that like the African mountain gorilla, trade unions have contracted mainly because their traditional fields of organisation have severely declined, as in the workforces of many of the bastions of trade union strength such as coal mining, ship building, steel and textiles. This has, of course, been linked to an evident failure by trade unions in Britain and elsewhere to break out of their traditional pastures, as in the 'smokestack' industries, and establish themselves in the new and rapidly-expanding employment industries, from electronic data processing to fast food.

The environmental view of the 'shrinking habitat' is clearly borne out by recent Labour Force surveys which show that trade union density is still highest in the most rapidly contracting industries such as coal mining (91 per cent), and at its lowest in many of the new industrial sectors ranging from 'cleaning services' (16 per cent), 'electronic data processing' (10 per cent), and 'take away food shops' (1 per cent).[2]

In addition, trade unions have clearly been affected by the severe and continuing shrinkage in the British manufacturing sector, now in 1993 some 25 per cent smaller by any objective measure than in 1980. Within manufacturing industry, trade unionism was and remains strong across the board, from motor vehicle manufacture and heavy engineering through to food, drink and tobacco. In these areas recent Labour Force surveys also show that trade union *density* has actually remained high, but set, of course, against a background of rapidly contracting employment where plant closures and mass redundancies have become almost daily occurrences.

One leading industrialist of the 1980s, Sir Ian MacGregor, recently claimed (and evidently without shame) to have alone presided over the elimination of some 250,000 industrial (and therefore, mainly trade union) jobs, proudly stating 'Nobody got fired—I simply exploited the British Syndrome which is "How soon can I stop working!"'.[3]

So the erosion of their traditional fields of recruitment has unarguably been the major factor in accounting for the trade union decline in Britain in the last decade. In addition, evidence suggests that the six successive rounds of 'Employment' Legislation (in fact mainly directed at restraining

[1] *Department of Employment Gazette*, April 1991.
[2] *Incomes Data Services Report 621*, July 1992.
[3] *Guardian*, 22 September 1992.

unions) which Britain's Conservative Government has enacted since 1979, have unquestionably added to the difficulties of trade unions by making it more difficult for them to survive the offensives of hostile employers, let alone break out of their traditional confines, to recruit new 'greenfield' members and obtain recognition from new employers.

Human resource management

The changes in the composition of the U.K. workforce, aggravated by a framework of Employment Law unquestionably more hostile than any in the rest of Europe, have been the main elements responsible for the decline in size and influence of what was once generally acknowledged to be the most cohesive trade union movement in the western world. What then of new managerial techniques?

There are certainly those, including some influential groups within the trade union movement both in Britain and elsewhere who have suggested that increasingly used new management techniques have had, as part of their hidden agenda, the objective of constraining and marginalising trade union influence in business enterprises, if not eradicating it absolutely. Such views have, in the recent past, been articulated by some fairly influential figures in the British trade union movement, particularly on the Left. In recent times, however, the British TUC and the majority of its affiliated trade unions have tended to take a more pragmatic view. With the obvious exception of an apparently growing fashion for 'union busting', unions now tend to view new managerial methods with less suspicion, and show a willingness to work with and within the changed systems of work organisation which often flow from the application of HRM techniques. The reasons for this evident shift in the trade union position I will examine later.

First, why has British industry embraced new management theories and techniques so enthusiastically in recent times? After all, many of the major studies of Britain's economic decline have highlighted the shortcomings and innate conservatism of much of British management (as well as its workforce) and have generally criticised the unwillingness of British industry to embrace new techniques, philosophies and products as well as Britain's 'adversarial' system of industrial relations. Perhaps this view was always a little unfair. In the early years after the publication of the Donovan Report,[4] in my experience as a researcher and subsequently a working trade union official, it was commonplace to meet British managers at all levels who would readily defer to Fox's 'pluralistic' model of industrial relations,[5] if only too often to add 'but of course in this firm we're all in this together, one big happy family'.

[4] *Royal Commission on Trade Unions & Employers Associations*, H.M.S.O., London, 1968.
[5] Alan Fox, *Industrial Sociology & Industrial Relations—Royal Commission Research Paper No. 3*, H.M.S.O., London, 1968.

But whatever shortcomings there may be in the contemporary British management, an unwillingness to embrace new ideas is no longer one of them. In fact, managerial 'big ideas' and new managerial techniques seem to have become the new industrial Holy Grail. In a way, the wheel has turned full circle and we appear today to have returned, through HRM, to the 'one big happy family' view of the enterprise, at least in the eyes of senior managers and their advisers.

Let me make clear that when I talk of *management techniques* here, I am not talking simply of systems like HRM, but the whole spectrum of managerial approaches to the workforce ranging from outright American-style 'union busting' through to total or partial derecognition of trade unions. Finally the term 'management techniques' encompasses a range of management systems which are directed towards such issues as customer service or product quality. The latter owes a great deal to United States and Japanese influence and managerial philosophies, though often, it must be said, greatly bastardised and with aspects such as 'lifetime commitment' conveniently jettisoned in their long journey from the Pacific Rim.

These US and Japanese-inspired systems include 'Total Quality Management' (TQM) and other product and service quality-related techniques such as 'Just In Time' systems, through to more generalised and people-orientated approaches seeking to motivate the workforce, in which concepts such as 'flexibility' and 'teamworking' are paramount. The importance of 'communication' and 'briefings' as a means of employee involvement is invariably a further major element in such schemes. These systems as developed by various consultants and applied by different firms are of infinite variety; but in so far as they tend to embody most of the foregoing elements, it is convenient to group them together under the 'HRM' label.

A number of factors have obviously played their part in encouraging British management to look for new methods. First of all, as is well known, what is left of British manufacturing industries faces increasing competition within global markets, and is forced to examine and often to emulate the techniques of its major overseas competitors in its struggle to survive. A high profile example of this would be the metamorphosis of what is now the Rover Car Manufacturing Group (formerly the troubled British Leyland Company), which in its slimmed-down form, has in recent years publicly embraced many of the manufacturing methods of its Japanese competitors as well as those of its partner, Honda. There is no evidence of any significant trade union opposition to this within the Rover Group. Indeed, the national leadership of the Amalgamated Engineering Union has been recently prepared to declare publicly that such changes were essential and inevitable for the survival of the company.

A further example of this change, from the motor industry, in a traditional area of trade union militancy, Merseyside, was seen when local union representatives at Vauxhall were prepared in 1990 to accept a fundamental revision of the agreements on working practices in return for a guarantee from General Motors in that their new European V6 Engine plant would be built in Ellesmere Port rather than located abroad. In this case, it was claimed by local unions that they had, by negotiation, resisted what they regarded as excessive managerial initiatives on such issues as 'team working' (a common feature of HRM systems), with its stress on 'continuous improvements' in quality and output and changing employee attitudes. By doing this the Vauxhall Unions on Merseyside claimed to have ensured a continuing union influence in working processes, as well as resisting a total divorce from national pay bargaining and a move to more localised reward systems.

Traditional areas of motor industry trade union militancy such as Merseyside might, even by the late 1980s, have been thought to be fertile ground for the philosophies of opposition to HRM which had previously emerged in the American United Automobile Workers Union (UAW), where an influential section had argued for outright union opposition to team working in the motor industry on the grounds it was 'management by stress'.[6] But in the Ellesmere Port case, pragmatism clearly won the day. A locally-based study conducted by union-based organisations concluded:

> 'The unions decided that negotiated change is preferable to imposed change; if the new contract was rejected out of hand, it could be imposed at some point in the future with worse consequences the union believed.'[7]

Industrial relations in the British Motor Industry have traditionally had the highest media profile of any sector (with the possible exception of the Newspaper Industry itself). Consequently, the widespread adoption in the motor industry in recent times of what have been called 'Japanese' working methods have been the most widely documented in the press. However, this publicity should not be taken to mean that the British Motor Industry have necessarily had the most fundamental changes in management style and methods.

An even more profound change in managerial philosophies has occurred in the past decade in what was once Britain's public sector. It flowed from the government's extensive privatisation programme, which has now transformed most of the nation's former utilities and public sector undertakings operated on 'public service' principles to market-facing commercial organisations accountable to their shareholders.

This transformation in ownership from public to private has unquestionably brought about a sea change in managerial systems and attitudes in these enterprises from board level down. Most have devoted massive amounts of time and resources to changing what were often very conservative and rigid management hierarchies wedded to public service

---

[6] P. B. Beaumont, 'Trade Unions and HRM', *Industrial Relations Journal*, Vol. 22, No. 4, 1991, p. 304.
[7] *Trade Union responses to new Management Techniques*, Centre for Alternative Industrial and Technological Systems, and Merseyside Trade Union Centre, 1991.

principles. Considerations of cost and profit usually took a minor place in relation to other goals.

In my own experience, as a working trade unionist operating in a company which was included in the Thatcher Government's first wave of privatisation, British Telecom plc (BT) (formerly the nationalised Post Office Telecommunications Business) has offered a classic example of this sea-change in management styles. In BT's case, the transformation from public monopoly to competitive enterprise has brought about profound changes in both management style and the attitudes of the work-force. The old nationalised Post Office, of which BT was once part, in my view embodied much of what was best in Britain's public service tradition. Its management was in the main 'drawn from the ranks'. In the early years after privatisation in 1983, BT's management board appeared to wish to sample every conceivable managerial philosophy of the last 50 years (and some pretty inconceivable ones). Eight years ago the office bookshelf of the average senior BT manager ranged from the self-improvement volumes of Dale Carnegie to the technocratic tomes of Peter Drucker, together with a prospectus for the latest managerial Outward Bound course, entailing managers spending a night on a wet Welsh mountain! In recent years this eclectic approach has sensibly been abandoned in favour of a more coherent strategy embodying classic HRM ingredients:

A Company Mission Statement
In BT's case—
'To become the most successful Worldwide Telecommunications Group'.
[The so-called 'Top Telco' strategy]
plus
'*A Statement of (BT) Values*'
'We put our customers first
We are professional
We respect each other
We work as one team
We are committed to continuous improvements'[8]

This approach has been coupled with a massive shake-up of BT's internal management and organisational structures. This has included the 'de-layering' of management (another currently fashionable nostrum) and has seen some 15,000 managerial posts disappear in the period between 1990 and 1992. A further product of privatisation has been a substantial dismantling of much of the machinery of joint consultation. Motivated by the nostrum that 'Management must manage', the old joint Union-Management consultation machinery was often seen as an obstacle to change, and the new style management were resentful of what they believed to be delaying tactics and obstructions to change by the trade union side at both national and local level.

[8] *Putting Customers First—A Guide to the new BT*, BT plc, 1991.

The kind of changes and new management philosophies adopted by the board of BT would appear to have been replicated in a range of privatised undertakings such as British Airways and British Gas. Such changes have unquestionably led to a major culture shock for junior managers and an even greater one for the trade unions concerned, whose own roots, traditions and values reflected those of the public sector and, frequently, the Civil Service.

Thus, in the past decade, trade unions in Britain have found themselves forced to cope with a massive change in their environment. A long period of relative industrial stability gave way to an era in which management attitudes to their workforce altered fundamentally: one in which unions have been seen, at best, as something of an irrelevance in an era of 'shared values', and, at worst, as obstructions to necessary change and 'flexibilty', opponents or enemies to be contained or, in some extreme examples, eliminated by such techniques as 'union busting'.

Union busting

I realise that the reference to 'union busting' as a 'new' technique may be greeted with some surprise, for the driving out of, or resistance to, trade unions by employers is surely at least as old as the century. It is, however, the case that in post-war Britain unilateral action by employers to actually derecognise or expel trade unions is very much a phenomenon of the past decade. The Wapping conflict of the early 1980s following the decision of Rupert Murdoch's News International Group to derecognise the two print unions, the National Graphical Association (NGA) and the Society of Graphical & Allied Trades (SOGAT), prior to its move to a new London Docklands production plant, most notably springs to mind. But there have been other less well-publicised examples. In the Telecommunications Sector, for example, the steps taken by Mercury Communications to eliminate the presence of the Association of Scientific Technical and Managerial Staff (ASTMS) it had inherited from the Cable and Wireless Company and to resist further unionisation have recently been well documented.[9] Whilst this never gave rise to the open conflicts witnessed on the highway at Wapping, the author of 'Phone Wars' describes in some detail the techniques and inducements which were used to persuade individual employees to give up their collective representation and opt for some form of personal contract with the employer to keep unions out. The prevailing view appears to have been that the company 'would have more flexibility if we were non-union'. Mercury's clear model in its dealings with its workforce, right from the start, appears to have been the computer giant, IBM, whose resistance to trade unionism and its emphasis on a highly

[9] Keith Bradley, *Phone Wars—The Story of Mercury Communications*, Century Business, London, 1992.

DAVID NORMAN

individualistic philosophy in its workforce (linked to the pursuit of quality and customer service) is well known and now widely emulated by other employers, especially in the computing and communications sector.

Post-Wapping, other national newspapers in Britain have also been on the offensive against unions. For example, the National Union of Journalists (NUJ) has experienced derecognition 'by a thousand cuts': the use of personal contacts to oust collective agreements in a number of other national newspapers. Like other unions faced by this problem, the NUJ has failed in its attempts to resist the growth of personal contracts and *de facto* derecognition by either industrial or legal means. The loss of their legal appeal against derecognition in an action against Associated Newspapers[10] appears to confirm that an employer may take such action and terminate a collective agreement unilaterally, without fear of any legal consequences.

There is growing evidence that derecognition by *inducement* or pressure on individual employees to accept personal contracts in place of collective representation appears to have been most damaging to the presence of trade unionism in management grades. It should be remembered that one of the reasons for Britain's exceptionally high trade union density prior to 1980 was the way in which trade unionism extended upwards into management grades in the workforce.

Trade unionism in senior management grades was obviously at its most common in the Civil Service and in the major public sector enterprises, where executive and managerial grades up to the highest level had, for more than half a century, seen their entire range of conditions of service from pay to promotion procedures largely determined on a collective basis. As a result, we saw in Britain a fairly rare phenomenon, the foundation and growth of a number of highly effective and specialised management unions representing executives and managerial grades in public sector services. These included the Engineering and Managers Association (EMA) (whose core membership lies in the management grades in the Electricity Industry), and such groups as the Society of Telecom Executives (STE) in British Telecom. A decade ago, the latter were effectively responsible for representing and negotiating on behalf of all managerial grades up to Director level.

The ethos of the Thatcher era and the coming of privatisation in many of Britain's public sector services unquestionably brought a marked change in attitude at board level in many former public services towards the existence of trade unionism amongst managerial grades.

In many instances, there have been clear pronouncements by boards in the new privatised industries that trade unionism was no longer appropriate to management grades, when cultural changes post-privatisation had introduced new sets of customer service oriented goals. The move from

[10] *Wilson v Associated Newspapers*, 1990.

118

public to private sector also cleared the way for personal contracts incorporating commonplace private sector 'perks' such as cars and private medical insurance (which had been unknown in the public sector), not to mention massive salary increases at the most senior levels in the enterprise. Such inducements have been used regularly to encourage a movement from collective representation to personal contracts amongst former public sector managers. Less subtly, there is evidence that trade union membership amongst managers can be an effective barrier to any promotion. The impact of this trend on some management unions has been serious. For example, within BT, the Society of Telecom Executives (STE), which prior to 1980 represented virtually all tiers of management up to board level, is now effectively left with only the bottom two tiers of first and second line managers in membership, the remaining grades having succumbed to the inducements and pressures of the personal contract or having been eliminated by another fashionable technique: 'delayering'.

The 'corralling' technique

The 'freezing-out' of unions, as has been seen, can take many forms. A further example is the way in which some companies have in recent times pursued an approach first observed in the United States, in which union recognition is retained in existing establishments, but effectively excluded when new sites are opened, or when new acquisitions are made. (The so-called 'corralling' technique.) An example of such a strategy in operation in the mid 1980s was seen when the London Docklands Light Railway first opened. Legally, the Railway was an operating subsidiary of London Transport. Up to that time, trade unions had enjoyed a very strong presence in London Transport and British railways generally for most of the present century. Yet the Docklands Railway opened initially as a non-union undertaking, and subsequently the Electrical, Electronic, Telecommunications and Plumbing Union (EETPU) obtained limited recognition after a 'beauty contest' in which the established railway unions took second place. The long-established trades unions in British Telecom have also had a similar experience of repeated exclusion from any new company venture. BT has not recognised unions in any of the new subsidiaries it has acquired since privatisation in 1983, as part of its 'mission' to become 'Top Telco'. In particular, it refused to concede recognition in an alarm company, Telecom Security Limited, and a manufacturing company, MITEL.[11] BT sought to justify this stance on the grounds that the decision whether or not to recognise unions was a matter for the management of the subsidiaries themselves rather than an issue of corporate policy.

Thus major conflicts of the Wapping variety are still very much the

[11] Both these companies were later sold by BT in 1992.

exception in British industrial relations. However, there is little doubt that in recent times there has been a new management attitude towards trade unions and in some cases an offensive against them. Stimulated by the belief that an absence of trade unionism would assist in achieving currently desirable goals, including 'labour flexibility' and 'enhanced competitiveness' and, strengthened by a more favourable legal framework, a significant number of British employers have sought to engage in some measure of de-unionisation in the past decade.

A recent study of this phenomenon concluded that, whilst *complete* derecognition of unions by British employers was still rare, partial derecognition in multi-plant firms was much more common—'some 13 per cent of companies with recognised unions in 1984 had at least partial derecognition by 1990'.[12] The evidence to date is sufficient to indicate that a trend is running against the unions which, as yet, they have proved unable to check or to turn.

Human resource management—the union response

The initially suspicious and often openly hostile response of British trade unions to HRM in the early 1980s was well documented. It is clear that British union attitudes were shaped by the experience of trade unions in the United States where there appeared to be overt links between HRM and the anti-union movement. Unions undoubtedly mistrusted attempts to motivate employees to identify wholly with the aims and values of a company in circumstances where these were often linked to a campaign to persuade employees that trade union membership was neither necessary nor compatible with their commitment to the employer.

With the experience of the shrinking trade union movement in the United States very much in mind, a number of British trade union leaders viewed the application of HRM by employers with considerable mistrust, and were ready to articulate their misgivings. For example, in 1989 Ron Todd, then General Secretary of the Transport and General Workers Union (TGWU) characterised new management techniques in the following terms: 'a new era of crafty Rambo managers has come into existence, who seek to ignore or deliberately disrupt union organisation and collective bargaining procedures by bringing in their own schemes based on fake committees and centred on the individual worker, not the organised worker, with the aim of undermining established working practices and bargaining methods'.[13]

There is no doubt that these attitudes of suspicion can still be found in some sections of the British trade union movement, for example the

[12] P. Gregg & A. Yates, 'Changes in Wage Settling Arrangements and Trade Union Presence in the 1980s', *British Journal of Industrial Relations*, September 1991.
[13] *Employee Involvement and Quality Circles*, Transport & General Workers Union, 1989.

Labour Research Department (LRD), an influential independent trade union body, in a publication in August 1992 returned to the theme that HRM posed a threat to trade unionism by saying: 'Under HRM and TQM approaches, managers are encouraged to see themselves as people-managers whose priority is to directly motivate and win over the people under them. Trade union representatives may find themselves marginalised, as management, with superior resources, authority and time, set up new mechanisms for giving information to, and receiving information from, individual workers.'[14]

It must however be said that the views expressed by the TGWU and the LRD no longer appear to be the prevailing trade union approach to HRM in Britain. The TUC, in particular, now appears to be seeking actively to promote trade union involvement in the 'pursuit of quality' and to ensure that unions are involved in both the public and private sector. In a recent publication, the TUC, whilst including the customary *caveat* that 'management systems with quality as their driving force reach out to employees on an individual basis rather than a collective basis, may have negotiated *with* the Unions, but are rarely *controlled* by them',[15] then goes on to argue for a 'partnership approach' to achieving service quality in which 'the union input is acknowledged and credited by staff and management'. This view has been echoed by the leaders of many of Britain's largest unions in recent times. This pro-active approach by many British trade unions to HRM echoes a philosophy laid out with great clarity by Lord McCarthy in a paper presented to a special TUC Consultative Conference in May 1991 on the future of trade unionism.[16] In proposing an agenda for trade unionism in the 1990s, McCarthy actually set a specific goal for trade unions 'humanising' HRM. He sought to link the underlying philosophy of HRM with the essential principles of trade unionism. In his contribution to the Conference he said:

'the fashionable umbrella term to refer to systematic attempts to raise performance and commitment is "Human Resource Management" or HRM. The slogan of HRM aficionados is "People Count". Most workers, whether unionised or not, adopt a somewhat sceptical attitude towards the threatened advance of many HRM techniques; but it is important to realise that there is a sense in which it derives from managerial acceptance of a truth that has always been a basic tenet of trade unionism. People at work ought not to be regarded as another factor of production; they are human resources, which needs to be motivated in ways that command respect and attention.'

Evidence of that philosophy in practice is also shown in the TUC General Council's own subsequent proposals, which included training trade union officials and lay members the better to respond to and sometimes take the initiative in HRM schemes.

---

14 Labour Research Department, August 1992.
15 *The Quality Challenge*, Trades Union Congress, 1992.
16 *TUC Towards 2000—A Consultative Document*, May 1991.

Recent years have seen significant moves towards decentralisation and flexibility, particularly in the public sector, and strategies informed by the latest 'human resource management techniques'. While some of these moves may be a reaction to a particular economic and political climate, and change as the climate changes, there nevertheless seems to be a fundamental shift. Through an extensive programme of seminars at national and regional level, the TUC has been studying how to develop an active rather than reactive response to these developments i.e., envisaging them as a means of opening up areas of employee choice, giving them more influence over their working lives and enhancing their jobs, status and career opportunities.

The presence of the Director General of the Confederation of British Industry as a guest speaker to the 1992 Trades Union Congress for the first time in its 124 year history was rightly seen as a significant signal from the leadership of the British trade union movement. It signified above all that, in the aftermath of the General Election earlier in the year and the election of a Conservative government for its fourth term, trade unions have accepted that they must live in the world as they find it and not as they might wish it to be. Of course, such philosophy is not new, for 'New Realism' was being actively promoted by a number of influential trade union leaders in the mid 1980s. The most recent development (post the 1992 General Election) could reasonably be characterised as 'New Realism—Mark II'. The growing willingness of trade unions to get involved in HRM and other related issues in a positive way can thus be seen as a facet of the latest round of 'realism'.

At the outset I posed the question as to whether there was anything 'new' about the so-called 'new management techniques' such as HRM. Clearly the desire of employers to motivate their workforce to work harder and turn out quality products is as old as the industrial process itself. Against this historical background the 'new' management techniques for motivating workers can perhaps be seen simply as part of a long tradition stretching back, if not to the 'Carrot and Stick' approach of Taylor and the Piecework Revolution, then, at least, to the 1920s and industrial philosophies derived from Elton Mayo's work, sometimes crudely characterised as 'Better Milk From Contented Cows'!

I referred earlier to the fact that, in one sense, practitioners of Industrial Relations like myself have seen the wheel turn full circle in a generation. The 'unitary' models of the commercial enterprise and its participants, which were discarded as unfashionable in the early 1970s (which I described earlier as the 'one big happy family approach') are not dissimilar from the underlying philosophies of HRM, with its promotion of 'mission statements', sets of 'shared values' which now purport to link all participants within an enterprise: managers and managed and shareholders together in a common bond.

There is no doubt that much of British management today in every sector is actively promoting (and, incidentally, spending a great deal of money) on a variety of HRM techniques. Many, if not all, entail regularly

122

gathering groups of employees together for some form of 'team briefing' which seek to reinforce the employee's commitment to the firm. It is perhaps surprising that, to my knowledge, so little has been done to assess how much of this philosophy actually permeates the sensibilities and influences the behaviour of basic grade employees in the longer term. An independent study carried out on behalf of my own union revealed (comfortingly for us, perhaps) that employees were five times as likely to trust information given to them by their union than that provided by the employer. It is communication problems such as these that management is seeking to address with HRM; but it must be said that, in my experience, HRM techniques are often received at best with suspicion and often mocked at shop floor level. HRM is generally perceived as a 'foreign' import and therefore perhaps inevitably meets with a measure of cultural resistance. Given the traditions of the British workforce and the structure of our far from 'classless' society, there is also inevitably a tendency amongst workers to show a healthy scepticism when it is suggested within any company that the interests of the shareholders, the £350,000 a year Chairman of the enterprise and the £15,000 a year manual worker are always identical. And that perceived existence of a divergence of interest will surely continue to remain part of the fundamental *raison d'etre* for trade unions.

Within the environment they find themselves and against the background of the new realism, trade unions will no doubt continue to involve themselves in new management initiatives and techniques, just as they have sought to influence a wide variety of management systems of the past. Trade unions *must* do this, less their worst fears are fulfilled and they see themselves marginalised by the promotion of philosophies in the work place that present the role of the individual as paramount, to the exclusion of all others. The trade union response to new management techniques is, therefore, conditioned by the desire to survive in the territory which they still hold. Quite how they break out of their rapidly-eroding natural habitat and expand into new ground is, of course, another issue entirely.

To end up, perhaps appropriately, in my own backyard, let me return to that statement of BT Values, quoted earlier:

We put our customers first
We are professional
We respect each other
We work as one team
We are committed to continuous improvements.

In the early summer of 1992, BT sought for a variety of reasons to 'downsize' its workforce. It called for in the region of 15,000 volunteers to leave the company, offering, it must be said, a not unreasonable package of financial inducements.

Something in the region of 95,000 employees initially expressed an interest in leaving the company. One might ask, if the commitment to 'shared values' was as great as the employer had hoped, why was there such a great desire amongst BT's employees to depart from the company? Again this might seem to add weight, perhaps, to my scepticism concerning the impact of HRM techniques on the workforce. In further support of this view, I proffer the example of the sacking of Lord Hall, the then Post Office Chairman, by the incoming Conservative Government in 1971. Hall's sacking, as Chairman, actually led to spontaneous industrial action in the form of 'walk outs' and strikes by both postmen and telephone engineers, and there was a great deal of union clamour and protest against the enforced removal of a popular Chairman. With the best will in the world, I have to say that I could not foresee a similar reaction amongst the workforce were Mr. Iain Vallance to be removed from his post as Chairman of BT today. The fact is that, for all its faults, including its unquestionable inflexibility in meeting customers' needs, the old Public Sector enterprise did actually embrace, in large measure, a unitarist culture: a wide range of shared values existed amongst its workforce. Paradoxically, for all that has been spent on HRM and other management nostrums in the past decade, those shared values, in my experience, have actually been eroded since privatisation, and are well on the way to extinction.

This view is, I know, wholly subjective; but perhaps adds weight to the conclusion that the real impact of HRM on the workforce in Britain has still to be truly assessed and properly evaluated.

Conclusion

I would conclude that most of the fashionable management techniques of the past 10 years, and in particular HRM, have not yet proved themselves readily transplantable to British shores, and will perhaps always be of questionable value because of cultural factors unique to the UK workforce. Frankly, I see them as unlikely to be of lasting value as a means of raising employee commitment to the firm. indeed, the widespread extent of privatisation in the UK and the perceived inequalities that have flown from these changes have probably eroded the 'shared values' which once existed between managers and managed. What measure are likely to be effective in fostering the industrial co-operation still necessary for success is, of course, another question. But from the perspective of British trade unions, there is no doubt that the prospect offered by Jacques Delors, President of the European Commission, of a 'European' vision of industrial democracy and co-determination, one which fully recognises and prescribes a role for *collective* worker representation, clearly has its attractions for a trade union movement currently starved of influence and conscious of a decline which it has, as yet, proved unable to reverse. However, in my personal view, unions will have to come to recognise that in circumstances where they now represent fewer than one worker in three, the concept of the union as the 'single channel' for workers'

© The Political Quarterly Publishing Co. Ltd. 1993.

involvement, sought by the unions in the 1970s, is no longer appropriate. Any new systems of employee involvement in an enterprise must inevitably recognise that trade unions are only a minority voice in the workforce as a whole. They are, however, still, for the foreseeable future, a significant one and one which management would do well to take fully into account when planning for the future.

THE INFORMAL POLITICS OF THE EUROPEAN COMMUNITY

KEITH MIDDLEMAS*

In the third volume of my trilogy (1974–1990) about the informal side of British government since World War II, I argued that the unacknowledged face of politics—in particular the interchanges between politicians, civil servants, finance, industry and labour—had been ruptured during Mrs Thatcher's decade. The capacity, the positive or negative power of unofficial institutions to shape or frustrate what governments do, and influence their thinking in a cumulative way, had been seriously, but not however terminally, impaired. The question that remained was not whether that part of the political system that had been characterised for half a century by a measure of continuous informal bargaining, the 'dark side of the moon', had sustained irreversible change but whether it had either gone into temporary abeyance, or experienced a mutation 'lower down' and further from the centre.

Of course this reversal of an old trend had not been due only to Mrs Thatcher and her governments. It had begun in Britain in the mid-1970s crisis and had been facilitated by change in the social and economic role of trades unions, the Labour government's policy changes after 1976, and the increasing dominance of financial institutions world wide. Neither was Britain unique: like the welfare state and the doctrine of full employment, informal networks based on interest group power were eroded in European countries ranging from Sweden to Italy, while a seismic shift in policy concern from unemployment to inflation occurred in nearly all of them in the early 1980s. The decline of Keynesian macro-economic management, the dominance of money markets and financial institutions, the elevation of finance ministries over industry ministries, indicated the depth of this change.

Nothing that has happened under John Major inclines me to change that opinion. But I also argued that corporate bias and the informal political linkages typical of all developed polities up to then had survived, though temporarily exiled from Whitehall, below ministerial level, among a more complex range of players: the giant firm now mattered (more than the CBI which had become more of a civil service for British manufacturers), the multinational finance house, and even the high-skilled composite trade union. Opportunities for these to be heard in tripartite macro-economic

* Keith Middlemas is Professor of Contemporary History at the University of Sussex.

argument had virtually disappeared, as NEDC itself was to do in December 1992. But on a less grandiose agenda, at regional level, in the micro economy of industry and finance, and above all on the European Community stage, they had if anything more scope to exercise influence than in the early 1980s. This was especially true of matters to do with regulation or deregulation, mergers and takeovers, competition policy, state aid to industry, environmental questions or the labour market once the Single European Act had been signed in 1986.

The mid-1970s crisis which ended Britain's post-war era was equally traumatic for the EC, plunging it first into a *sauve qui peut* after the oil shock and then nearly nine years of disinflation and stagnation, barely relieved in the upturn of 1976–79. But the years 1983–84 produced a profound change, ending nearly two decades in which the EC had stood still. From this grew the Single European Act (SEA) due not only to Jacques Delors' appointment, crucial though that was, or the initiatives of key individuals such as Lord Cockfield and Tommaso Padoa-Schioppa working within or on the fringe of the Commission; not only to the initiatives of core EEC governments, Germany and France, Holland, Belgium and Italy, but also from below: that is, from financial sectors as well as central banks, and from those industrial firms which already saw themselves as European rather than strictly national champions. For these the Community had become otiose, parcelled out, unprofitable as an organism and unproductive. Given their primarily international outlook, the EC had become a constraint, not an opportunity—as Davignon and the industrialists of the European Round Table had argued since about 1981.

It is wrong therefore to portray the Single Market as the result only of Commission or intergovernmental initiative. Both formal and informal political players could see by 1984–85 that the EC needed to be revitalised, and that such modernisation could be a complex process in which both could work to mutual advantage. Of the twelve prime ministers perhaps only Mrs Thatcher signed the SEA imagining it to be purely an economic matter, directed from above by national governments. (Whether this consensus among the eleven continued all the way to Maastricht is another matter.)

The model of informal players in a multi-layered game, where exclusion is almost impossible and play moves from negotiation to compromise rather than victory (which I have called Competitive Symposium) applies to most modern states. Even in present-day Russia, such business organisations have for months enjoyed under the label of Civic Forum an influence over macro-economic policy with President Yeltsin's administration, and the fact that they are still so deeply involved in shaping the nature of the Russian state suggests that even if, or when, they lose their formal umbrella 'party' structure, they will retain very substantial informal producer group power. In a far less politicised and threatening matter, it applies to EC member states, the EFTA associates, and probably to Poland, Hungary, and Czechoslovakia.

But does it also apply to the EC as a whole? Community institutions provide a forum extraordinarily well adapted for bargaining, to a degree which would be almost impossible within a nation state with its long established institutions, administrative habits and legal systems. It is hard to imagine a nation state where everything, from the planning of legislation to its enactment, its implementation, the punishment of infraction, and even the scale of penalty is open to negotiation or diversionary strategies. If for no other reason, that suggests that the Community is not yet a complete state. But if the existence of well integrated politics is, in nations, a sign of maturity, indeed a precondition of full democratic participation, does its proliferation across Europe, however excessive at the moment, suggest that the Community is on the way to becoming a state, of a rather different order, whether or not it acquires an EC defence force, a foreign policy, a fully operative parliament and a federal constitution?

Informal politics and those who play on that shapeless field of course transcend supranational borders. Most, if not all giant firms or financial houses are structured to meet global competition and are only partly concerned with the separate elements in a triadic division of the world. But the EC does manage and regulate a substantial part of the political matrix and the rules under which they operate. They may or may not wish to see the Community enlarge to include former EFTA countries: the gathering movement of firms out of Switzerland after that electorate's negative vote on EC entry, however, suggests they do. But their perception of 'Europe' is very different from that of member states' permanent representative in Brussels, or the bureaucrats in DG3 (Single Market, and aid to industry) or DG4 (Competition policy). What the Community is tends to be constructed out of what the viewer sees.

At every level of the game, different strategies are available to different sorts and sizes of players. Formally all member states have equal status, but in the informal pecking order they can be arranged in three distinct ways: large and small states, northern and Mediterranean ones, core and peripheral. The Danish public's vote against Maastricht highlighted how a relatively small country's inhabitants can maintain their own essential perceived interests—something which the Danish government had already demonstrated was possible over EC packaging directives. The Dutch central bank's behaviour in aligning the guilder to the Deutsche Mark may have been a logical necessity, but gives it a modest degree of leverage, beyond what a small country could otherwise expect. The fact that the Belgians managed to get what is in effect privileged access for their three regions' representatives to EC institutions is regarded enviously by much larger German Länder like Bavaria and North Rhine Westphalia, who have now discovered that the route is not to be regarded as a precedent.

The same applies to the core-periphery argument. If one takes the EMS, there is clearly a DM core including the Belgian, Dutch and perhaps Danish currencies, together with the Austrian schilling, and the periphery (Greece, Ireland, Portugal). France is still close—but may not be so after the March election—Italy, Spain and Britain remain most uncertainly in the area between. There is probably no strategy available to the central banks of Portugal, Greece or Ireland which would give them greater informal weighting. But in the EC's external relations, power to affect the outcome does not depend on measurable economic quantities: it may have been true in the 1960s that only the big four could invoke the Luxembourg compromise in defence of essential national interests (except on relatively minor issues such as Luxembourg's retention of the parliament). But today Greece, a poor Mediterranean peripheral state, can up to now insist against all the others that Macedonia should not be recognised under that name. Yet at the time the Maastricht Treaty was negotiated, experienced commentators thought that the Luxembourg compromise had ceased to exist. Maastricht may indeed have limited the facility with which it can be used, but it is not yet certain, for example, that France will not invoke it or something very similar later in the Uruguay GATT round. On the other hand, as Britain found in June 1982, even a large state may not in fact be able to sustain the compromise without at least some other backing in the Council of Ministers.

Informality resides in the EC's basic structure and in the Treaty of Rome itself. But the tendency, as with any relatively new institution, is slowly to move from the informal to the formal, reducing confusion to rules, precedents and customs or conventions. From the point of view of German legalism or British formality, the fact that informality and negotiation flourish in Brussels is something to be deplored and if possible to be diminished. From an Italian or Spanish point of view, it allows for much renegotiation and outright evasion-by-delay. But since the Commission has to work with sovereign members, playing politics (as Stanley Baldwin once observed) like Alice playing croquet with flamingos, the flexibility inherent in custom and convention is an invaluable advantage.

It also gives substantially more power to the Commission than the national leaders in the 1960s would have been willing to concede. Within any Commissioner's powers lies a grey area of interpretation. If a senior Commissioner, say Sir Leon Brittan, decides to proceed against firms involved in some market-rigging exercise, he has a range of modes available from warning to reference to the Court of Justice. What an English judge would refer to as his 'canons of construction' guide him in how to construe and bring to bear the original Treaty's section, how seriously to take the case, whether to negotiate for compliance or seek exemplary punishment, bearing in mind that in the latter case too low a fine would be disregarded, one too high may impair a firm's performance. Competence here, like that of a judge, will be interpreted according to the rules, but as judges differ, so do Commissioners. On a larger scale, in the various directorates, there is no single EC will, only a variety of inter-pretations of what the EC should do in particular fields of competence to implement its statutes and long-term aims, as interpreted by individuals throughout the organisation according to their ethos and practice, often much lower down in the ranking order of officials than is the case with national administrations.

The Commission is as much a congeries of small civil services as a single whole, held together by a loose geography of buildings and its President Jacques Delors, whose informal network has been staffed over the last eight years to provide his office with instant information and continuous analysis. Yet even Delors' mastery of detail is limited and, his men being known, others can use them to insert their own messages to the centre of the centre. A host of lobbyists, pressures groups and corporate consultants hover round. The structure is surprisingly unsecret to anyone acquainted with Whitehall, but also unhierarchic, open to initiatives and influence at every level. National governments have their permanent staffs, regional governments—where these exists—have their offices, very large firms or banks, many cities, most major trade union confederations have their lobbies. UNICE speaks for employers Europe-wide, ETUC for trades unions. All these, and players who have a shorter run or a narrower case to argue have their own contacts in an administration which is as open to permeation as a Gruyere cheese.

Informality creates its own rules of demarcation and cooperation. Brussels still gives the impression of being ill-coordinated except where powerful Commissioners impose a certain style. But to take a recent example, DG3 (Leon Brittan) and DG4 (Martin Bangemann) have since 1986 evolved an efficient joint approach to overlapping issues of competition and standardisation within the Single Market which, as a means of overcoming an inherent rivalry, can be compared with what had been achieved by the British DTI's two semi-compatible halves after its first decade of experience 1970–79.

Despite its formidable appearance to outsiders, the Commission is actually surprisingly careful, not to say timid. A recent analysis of where proposals for legislation originate showed that the majority came from member states. Having bargained with the Council of Ministers, and now the European Council throughout its history, it is certainly not insensitive to the considerable informal powers of delay or frustration which national governments possess. Like the Treasury here, it looks from outside like an immense castle, well fortified against the world, but from inside it seems a tiny pill-box, beset by marauding hordes. Delors's lengthy defensive regrouping since the Danish and French votes makes the point, as do the many instances where directives have been toned down or modified by protocols and other hedging devices to make them more acceptable. There is a basic Commission strategy, reflected both in the form of the original Treaty and in the Maastricht exemptions, to get the maximum of agreement down on paper and trust to time, goodwill, change in conditions and Commission persuasiveness to win full consent over a period of years. In that long time scale, northern members' complaints about Mediterranean evasiveness, Mediterranean members' hostility to German or French aggressiveness are merely descriptive devices to

conceal the price regularly paid for underlying consent. British punctili-
ousness, say, over slaughterhouse standards seems to French or Spanish
eyes distinctly odd. (But then the ways that member states behave,
whether in running committees or arguing about the legal and political
niceties of the Single Market, constitute a distinct sub genre of informal
politics, research into which gives some substance to the old argument
about national characteristics.)

Conscious of being guardians of a grandiose but necessary set of aims,
yet unable to impose on member states what they are not willing to accept,
Commission officials have both to interpret what members wish as well as
what they ought to wish, and then seek to lead them at a pace which gives
sufficient momentum yet which leaves no one too far behind. The scope
for deals is endless, the networks infinite. Such deals positively invite big
organisations to participate. The Commission or its component DGs
indeed invite them in, knowing that they depend on them for information
about the markets they seek to regulate, using the consultation process to
give just enough in return to keep the flow going. Sometimes the producers
win, sometimes the Commission, sometimes the deal constitutes no more
than the lowest common denominator of agreement. But in general,
Commissioners seek to have such forces as the giant chemical companies
or motor car producers as part of the deal—in the celebrated words of
L. B. Johnson, they prefer them inside the tent pissing out, not outside
pissing in.

Some of these deals are, to British eyes, frankly corporatist and
defensive: the current state of argument over high definition colour
television and Japanese car imports being two cases in point. But deals are
not like laws, made to last forever. Within a set legal framework, they are
intended only to last until the next deal, when circumstances and needs
have changed. The underlying, unchanging element remains the Single
Market, and behind that the Treaty itself, so that the process is intended to
resemble a slave-collar: it tightens slowly, especially if the victim struggles,
but it does not subsequently relax.

Deals made on this basis need constant supervision and repair. A lax
Commissioner can undo five years of painstaking work by failing to spot
abuses, collusion, or evasion. The current GATT round would have been
easier had the Agriculture Directorate done something in the mid-1980s
about proliferation of oil seed rape; the budget would look better if it had
avoided the current scandal of EC tobacco growing. Deals endure because
of this incorporation of all potential interests, but equally easily become
cosy arrangements between poachers and gamekeepers. It is debatable
whether they change behaviour more quickly than would have been the
case had more stringent rules been passed in the first place. Yet that
implies a degree of coherence which is absent. (One of the surprising
factors about the Commission is how little collective long-term memory
has been codified in its various segments. Commercial memory is invariably short, that of governments usually cyclical. Like civil servants

131

elsewhere, Commission officials possess the informal power of information retrieval and selective presentation, but they are so few in relation to the workload that in practice they rely heavily on the other players.)

In turn, the giant firm or the peak organisation expects to be asked for advice and to participate as of informal right (making it the more surprising how few major British firms have permanent representatives in Brussels. A paid lobbyist on £1000 a month retainer is not the same thing as a consultant of proven influence maintained out of corporate pay-roll.) National interests still speak to 'their' nationals in any DG and most directors general accept or even encourage this, knowing that that is how things work, and preferring it to be out in the open, arguable and refutable.

British governments' habitual secrecy and legal formalism of course makes it harder to operate successfully in such an environment. They do best in the big set pieces, at Maastricht or Edinburgh, where administrative skills of round the clock briefing and back-up matter most. But in the interstices and cross-ways they do badly. Mrs Thatcher's downfall began in Rome in October 1989 when she was outmanoeuvred by the Florentine diplomacy of Guilio Andreotti. Other EC members never understood the Thatcherite virtue of banishing interest players, knowing that if barred frontally, their influence seeps in through back doors and underground passages. Better have them in the open like French farmers, Italian insurance houses, Spanish construction firms, or German Länder. The Gruyère cheese is a model, not a cautionary tale.

The obverse is that parliamentary democracy suffers, or more precisely is not allowed to intrude. To paraphrase Bagehot, 'we must not let the daylight in on mystery'. Thatcherite objections to informal influence look different in the managed politics of Brussels where on very complicated issues (corporate strategy, standards, competition policy, subsidies, pollution or training) knowledge, experience and committee room skills matter more than aggregates of votes. It is bound to be so, given that the EC's objectives are to achieve harmonisation and integration across Europe's internal boundaries, community of action outside them. In so far as the EC's informal politics help to ensure that the players work together they may in fact offset an existing democratic deficit for which member states and the Commission, ever jealous of a more powerful European parliament, are equally to blame.

How to describe a network which stretches into twelve member states, on at least five levels of interchange? (Commissions and governments, regions, corporate and commercial bodies, and national—but barely yet European—publics.) Last September's financial crisis and the partial collapse of EMS have to be read not only on the governmental level but also that of central banks and finance ministries (for the Bundesbank clearly wanted to help the lira and above all the franc more than it did sterling). Central bank governors have to play their game not only on the national level, but also on that of the EC's Monetary Committee and the EC's Committee of Governors meeting in Basel. It is not credible that all

132

twelve should give equal weight to each. Whatever the others' concerns, the Bundesbank focused on German domestic considerations, having always thought that the path to EMU should begin with a core group of currencies able to fulfil the criteria from the start. But this outlook was determined partly by the regional level, that is the votes of Länder representatives on the Bundesbank council, some of whom began to worry about the effect of EMU on the deutschmark shortly after Maastricht. Carlo de Benedetti was only the first of many industrialists to protest, on 18 September, that the rest of European industry was being crucified to pay the price of German unification.

A fissure runs across EC politics (as it has done in Britain since 1980) matching an old fault line, not between finance capital and industrial capital—a 19th century formulation—but between two distinct ways of running a capitalist economy: that of the Treasury and the Central Bank, as opposed to that of politicians, spending departments and industrialists. The provisions for the European central bank, embodied in the Maastricht Treaty, were left by the EC authorities almost entirely to the Committee of Governors to draft. In retrospect, some of the antipathy to Maastricht, and the likely long delay in achieving the EMU chapter, suggests a change in the balance between them since 1990. But the fixing of target dates may itself by an informal gesture, of no more than indicative value: the Single Market was originally scheduled for 1972.

Community history has oscillated between frenetic leaps and stagnation. After the leap of 1986, followed by another to Maastricht, we may be in for a period like the mid and late 1960s of bickering and obstructiveness associated then with de Gaulle. But the game is no longer in the hands only of national governments. Apart from internationally powerful industrial and financial players, a handful of regions have asserted that subsidiarity means taking appropriate decisions in their own centres of power, not in national capitals. In setting up the Committee of Regions the EC is conducting an experiment which may have substantial repercussions on those member states who do not, like Germany, Spain, Italy, Belgium or France already have a developed regional structure. Greece is beginning to do so, Britain has far to go.

But the regional game is only just starting. Regions vary hugely, some being nation states in their own right (albeit unacknowledged): Catalonia, Scotland. The so-called 'four motors' Lombardy, Catalonia, Rhône-Alpes, Baden-Württemberg, who collaborate extensively already, are relatively rich, with a spread of leading industry, services, including tourism and agriculture, and would have been weighty players anyway. If Calabria, Galicia and the other less developed recipients of the bulk of regional aid are included in the average, the Committee of Regions may never amount to more than the present Economic and Social Committee. The Commission has not laid down its status: that is for the informal game to indicate over the next decade. The possibilities range from being a lobby for more regional aid, a mechanism for modernisation, a way of

133

facilitating the Single Market by cross-border cooperation, to becoming a counterweight to the twelve nation states; and thus the means by which subsidiarity is subsequently defined. It is worth noting that under Jordi Pujol, Catalonia has already developed links with foreign countries which go beyond trade policy to a limited foreign policy; the Spanish government apparently accepts this, provided the initiatives are channelled through Spanish embassies. Some German Länder could claim the same.

The main differences between EC informal politics and those of the nation state lie in the greater range of alliances and modes of action available; and in the greater degree of legitimacy conceded to the various players' operations (which is itself one Commission answer to the democratic deficit). On airline deregulation, for example, a national champion like Air France will have a ready ally in its own government and probably in its own trade union movement, to say nothing of the public which can be stimulated to defend a key national interest. On takeovers and mergers, cross-border as well as single state combinations can be put together, while like will side with like, for example against aspects of the Social Chapter at Maastricht. Italian insurance companies band together with Rome's help against liberalisation of financial services, as do Spanish banks—only to find that, whereas they may have support from some departments in Madrid, the Bank of Spain ranks competition and modernisation together.

All the players are motivated by self-interest. It is hard to imagine that Delors II was not directly related to French fears at Germany becoming the dominant member after unification, just as Germany's early support for the SEA embodied a desire to limit the Community's excessive propensity to bargain and then reopen negotiations later. But the convention of competitive symposium requires that each also acknowledges a higher interest, if for no other reason than that if they do not, they remain liable to exclusion by others that do from participating in the very important argument as to what is the eventual national, and in this case, supranational interest. In the Single Market era it does no good to argue flatly against harmonisation; rather the firm or sector must argue, 'harmonise this way because it is more efficient, environmentally friendly, supportive of employment, encouraging to backward regions'. The cohesion fund may have been *au fond* a device to buy Spanish, Portuguese and Greek support for the onerous side of Maastricht, but the players in that game, even at Edinburgh, dressed it up in a higher European language.

For any player there is still a choice between arguing about a national interest and a European interest. (One way to measure how far a firm has begun to think strategically in European as well as national-international terms is to test this balance: something similar can be done for members of what may be turning out to be a European political class.) Most are prepared to show themselves modestly good Europeans because this is the easiest way to set an acceptable agenda, enlist sympathy in Brussels, and play to the Commission's need to have them in the negotiating framework. To volunteer advice may itself bring a player into the game, as the TUC succeeded in doing quite early on in the drafting of the Social Chapter.

If German negotiators often insist on precise legal formulations, this is not necessarily to be condemned as legalism: it may be an attempt to tie up all the loose ends and prevent the French or Dutch from opening it up again later. The British, believing in absolute parliamentary sovereignty, ought perhaps to be more sympathetic, given that the alternative is to prolong some processes almost indefinitely. Yet perhaps, being also pragmatic, they appreciate how essential flexibility is, how agreement after long bargaining may embody true consensus, and how, like treaties, deals between sovereign entities—at whatever level—last only so long as they have value to all who sign them. This makes plain an old paradox: how, despite latent economic power, Germany has on the whole done worse out of Community politicking than France, often with a weaker hand; and indeed worse than Benelux or Italy.

But it matters to accept the convention that there is, somewhere, a tangibly European good. Greece risks playing a nakedly self-interested hand too often, as Britain did in the early 1980s and has perhaps done in the last year. This is something which France always and Spain so far have rather skilfully avoided. At company level, the balance may be much more difficult, since a firm may put too many real resources into the European project to the detriment of its international competitiveness. Among the leading European champions of the 1980s, whose empires had expanded very largely in that context for example, four Italian concerns, Fiat, Olivetti, Pirelli and Feruzzi (the agro-industrial group) are now seriously over-committed or endangered.

The European Parliament remains the weakest, most ill-coordinated player, and not only—as MEPs endlessly complain—because of its still inadequate formal powers. It had some role in making Maastricht because of its President's access to the Commission and because it could play on a certain sense of guilt about the democratic deficit. It has certainly benefited from the vigour of MEPs representing the most active and ambitious regions, like North Rhine Westphalia and Bavaria. But it is also a sounding board for regional groups anathema to central governments (e.g. Lega Nord members, separatists from the Basque country and Corsica), who try to use EC institutions as a way to legitimate their struggles. There is a very long way to go before national groupings of Christian Democrats or Social Democrats will regard the European Parliament as the Conservative Party in the Commons used to regard the House of Lords.

One reason for this weakness in a forum which in theory could benefit from informal links with unelected players is that the parliament has so far very largely ignored its putative educational role. It has done little to publicise the Community's common good, or its long goals, in order to help foster a European public awareness. No other body has such an interest; most have an interest in retaining strictly national publics. The European public may never come about through political umbrellas such as the Parliament, given the fissiparous state of Christian democracy and social democracy in different member states, but only through the struggle of broad social groupings to express a deeply felt but inchoate interest, transcending national constraints. Among these may be listed the *pensionat*, whose huge and growing numbers have more in common across national boundaries than any other comparable group. A possible alternative is for the Parliament to lapse into a congeries of largely regional representatives, if that level of Community politics really develops.

The Community is not in any obvious sense a state. It has no full parliament: its authority is divided (and the last six months of 1992 showed how inadequate the Presidency is as an executive instrument when members are unwilling to follow its leadership); it does not rest on a European public. Its citizenship consists merely of certain advantages or rather privileges, and few rights except for certain categories of people such as voyagers or those in work. It has no armed services, no single police. Yet it has a legal system, a court, an administration, a single external border, a sort of cabinet; it has the possibility of a central bank, fuller citizenship, a stronger parliament.

Formally it has therefore the makings of a state. Informally, it already possesses a system more complicated and just as sophisticated as exists in any modern nation, and elements of a political class at the European centre, capable of and eager to operate it. Under the Single Market regime, Commissioners and officials already see their role as shaping national requirements to European tendencies, rather than meeting the demands of actual national governments; in that sense the SEA may already have been a more significant transforming force than the making or modifying of Maastricht.

Even irreducible national minima seem more soluble than in the 1960s or early 1980s quarrels. French objections to GATT have so far, against most predictions, been turned back on themselves; Greek opposition to Macedonian recognition is already being undermined (though largely because of American rather than EC impatience). The Danes and Spanish have been bought off at Edinburgh by a mixture of blandishments, bargains and informal blackmail which looks at this stage to have been both collectively European and surprisingly successful.

In a more subtle way, the EC is becoming an example. Long years of experience of the Coal and Steel Commission, Euratom and the CAP taught participants in basic industry and agriculture as well as departments of state how to bargain across national borders, lessons they still employ. The cooperation of finance ministers and central bankers on the ECMonetary Committee or on the Governors Committee has done more to modernise national banking practices since 1980 than any single government could have achieved on its own. It is at least possible that the

EC's experience of statehood may be a transforming force for an Italy overrun with maladministration and corruption. Certainly many Italians see Brussels as a *point d'appui* not available inside their own country.

One outcome of the Cassis de Dijon case, an early judgment in Commission history, was a presumption about fewer strict rules and more room for negotiation. Similar battles seem to have gone the same way in the last year, over things as disparate as waste disposal and transport pollution. Whenever the Commission seems to overstep some hidden margin of tolerance, it is forced to abandon its leading role and resume the endless round of brokerage and bargaining. (The leading role may however itself be only a gambit designed to draw the 'opposition's' fire.)

It is reasonable to assume that the interplay between formal mechanisms and informal ones will continue, within a general tendency common to all political artefacts for the informal ones to become formalised over time (like COREPER and the European Council); and for new flexible ones to develop as well. A system exists, based on voluntarily accepted rules of engagement, convention and custom, without which it is hard to imagine Brussels could work at all. One of the pre-conditions for participation is that players have to accept both an element of European identity and some idea of a general European good, which may or may not coincide with their global outlook. Out of such understandings and experiences, new sorts of states are born.

WHITHER GLOBAL CAPITALISM?

WILL HUTTON*

So the collapse of communism has seen not just the end of history but the end of geography. We live in a world of similar liberal capitalist democracies compelled by necessity and interest to increase their collaboration in order to make the world even more free-market oriented, runs the argument. The industrialised democracies will develop ever more effective institutions of policy coordination to serve their mutual interest in free trade, sound money and economic harmonisation—building upon the trends already evident.

But are the trends towards collaboration or competition? Plausibly the Cold War masked the degree of competition between the industrialised capitalist countries by grouping them all in the same camp. But beneath the language of western solidarity existed strong national rivalries; and these are more rather than less likely to emerge over the years ahead. Only by recognising what is going on are there good chances of building durable institutions of international collaboration; but setting impossible targets for behaviour is likely to be both disappointing and self-defeating.

The thesis of the end of history or of geography is familiar. We live in an essentially if not wholly free-trade world which is moving imperfectly towards that end; attempts at protection have proved self-defeating for those countries which have tried it, whether France or Burma. Equally, in the realm of finance, if national governments want to attract capital then they must have stable prices; and to have stable prices requires a sound money policy. That means in turn there has to be constrained public expenditure and public borrowing, so that lowering ambitions for social programmes to the lowest common denominator becomes common policy.

The injunction goes very deep. For state economic activity generally is not going to be competitive with this world of trans-national and multi-national companies whose products are highly competitive. So state-owned car companies or state-owned steel companies, or any attempt by the state to get involved itself in economic activity is bound to be self-defeating; thus both India and Pakistan are engaged in massive privatisation programmes. Privatisation is described as a global trend to marry with the global trend to being unambitious about social provisions, to constrain budget deficits, to try and dismantle exchange controls and to open economies. It is a borderless world. It is the end of geography.

---

* Will Hutton is Economics Editor of *The Guardian*.

I want to dispute that thesis, even though it was the way American economists and strategists—and to a less extent their British counter-parts—in the planning departments of multi-national banks and corpora-tions certainly saw the world in the mid and late 1980s. But it did not correspond to the actual state of the world at that time. It was a particular set of circumstances that allowed all this to take place; and we should be aware of that particularity.

In short it was the culmination of a period starting in the early 1950s and which finished in the late 1980s, which has been characterised as the Cold War world. It masked national ambitions and a whole spectrum of varieties of capitalism; and we are not now going to surrender to the new conception of a borderless world. History and geography are very much with us and discovery of that over the next few years will compel the need to re-design a stabler and less asymmetric architecture of world trade and finance. Until then we will see more anarchic breakdowns of trade and financial relations, probably continuing stagnant world output and a growing consensus that change is necessary. The hidden hand of the market cannot, after all, end geography for us. Indeed geography never ceased.

Let us start with the Bundesbank—a quintessential Cold War institu-tion. Its period of success from 1957 through to German reunification in 1989 was a period in which it was almost able to define itself as having virtually no international obligations. It was the third leg of a dialogue in German policy-making. The first was Bonn; the second was the social partners, in particular industry-wide trade unions and industry-wide trade associations; and finally there was the Bundesbank.

The Bundesbank was concerned about the growth of broad money in Germany. By firing a shot by raising the Lombard rate, and in its early days actually physically raising the controls on the German banking system, it was able to secure lowered wage claims or lowered public expenditure or whatever was the most favoured combination in a domestic compromise. That broke down completely after the Cold War. There is no doubt that Theo Waigel, the German Finance Minister, and Chancellor Kohl now want to cap expenditure in the East; but it is not just the 200 billion DM of current transfers to Eastern Germany that have confronted the Bundes-bank. It is also the continuing transfers to the Russians to pull their troops out of Eastern Germany. It is the underwriting of export credit guarantees to support trade with Central and Eastern Europe. Germany also has obligations to the European Community and Bonn cannot cut its con-tributions to the EC budget. So the Bundesbank pitched the Lombard rate at 9.75 per cent, but still Bonn would not come to order. It is hardly surprising in the circumstances, and as Central-Eastern Europe opens up to reproduce the circumstances of inter-war years, some of the ghastly things that produced the great inflations of Germany are staring the Germans in the face.

Equally the Franco-German alliance is a Cold War phenomenon. Even

139

if the Germans are now claiming the leadership of Europe, throughout the Cold War France legitimately claimed that leadership; partly because it was at least as populous and powerful in terms of gross domestic product as West Germany, but secondly because the Germans did not hold nuclear weapons and had lost the war. Community leadership naturally fell to the French. For them the EC was coterminous with the French leadership of Europe. France was greater Europe. French was the language of Brussels and that was the reason why the French political classes adhered to the whole of the integration project. They were leading it.

Italian politics mirrored the Cold War rivalry. The whole point about Italian politics was to exclude the Communists from power, and that is why the political system paradoxically was stable even though it was unstable. This has now come to an end.

American industrial policy was built around the Pentagon and US arms expenditure; and even in terms of internal American political cohesion, the Cold War was very important. It could entrench Presidential power, while the role of the National Security Council became more and more significant. Trade and financial relations all pulled in the same direction. One of the reasons why the electronics industry in the US became so integrated with the defence industry was because of the Cold War imperative of winning the arms race.

Japan, spending one per cent of GDP on defence and with its protection underwritten by the USA was also a major beneficiary from the Cold War. Lack of defence expenditures, trade relations, the growth of a consumer electronics industry, were all interlinked with the US's geo-political aims. The American willingness in turn to run big bilateral trade deficits with Japan was centrally bound up with the Cold War order. The West was willing to co-operate and to keep this order on the rails in opposition to the Communist bloc, which was perceived to be extraordinarily dangerous, particularly in the 1950s and early 1960s.

So this end of geography in which multi-nationals and capital can move freely around actually derived from a Cold War order, and a willingness of states to subordinate national priorities to the larger goal of forming a Western interest. It started in the early 1950s, but it was clear by the early 1970s that the capacity to run the system and, for example, for America to underwrite the role of the dollar, had collapsed. Enter floating exchange rates.

The destabilising effects of financial freedom

What has happened as a result of the 1970s and 1980s is that financial intermediaries and financial institutions have increasingly been able to take advantage of this new capital market structure much more quickly than those engaged in the 'real economy'. New financial freedoms were offered at the same time as western states kept the system open for geo-political reasons. As a result there has been a seismic shift in the balance of power between finance and industry, tilting very much towards finance, especially in the Anglo-Saxon world. This is evident in the destabilisation of the foreign exchange markets after the collapse of Bretton Woods; but also with the rise of merger and acquisition takeover in both Wall Street and London.

Carrying the process forward through financial deregulation has meant that both the Bank of England and the Federal Reserve have lost control of the monetary aggregates, so that we have had a destabilising credit boom and bust in both countries. The rises and falls of the dollar in the foreign exchange markets have not just been a matter of financial concern. They have produced major structural imbalances in the distribution of production in the capitalist economies. Bluntly, the United States and Britain have overinvested in financial services and consumer services and not their internationally traded goods sector, while the Japanese have vastly overinvested in internationally traded goods.

Every year from 1986–1989 Japan's investment as a proportion of GDP was actually equivalent to the whole of France's GDP. It increased its capital stock by 50 per cent in four years and its capacity to produce cars, televisions, VCRs etc. multiplied above any likely market—giving a glut of productive capacity and confronting Japan with acute problems of adjustment. Japan will weather the structural adjustment with the remarkable set of institutions it possesses, but only by displacing problems onto the rest of the world.

It is ironic. Supporting US aims for the dollar, first by low interest rates and then buying dollars as a response to American blackmail over defence led to cheap capital that encouraged investment; and at the same time the high cost of capital in Britain and America led to disinvestment in the international traded goods sector and overinvestment in consumer services, property and banking. Thus the world economy is left with major structural imbalances, while at the same time people believe it is the consequence of the end of geography.

Equally 'the end of geography' has led to a systematic deflationary bias in the way in which countries can prosecute macro-economic policy. It forces them to push towards price stability and minimal social cost as the precondition of attracting international investment. Ireland competes with the North of Ireland which competes with Spain which competes with Scotland, driving down, for example, redundancy terms or the terms of product remittances. This forces governments to trim their expenditure at the same time as narrowing their tax base.

We are watching a systematic deflationary bias in policy whether it be in Sweden, which is having to move back from being a social democratic state, or in the rest of the EC coming to terms with the ERM and convergence terms for monetary union. The Nordic states are all deflating, dismantling their social democratic structures and embarking on deflationary policies to conform with the monetary union treaty. It is a European deflation.

141

But paradoxically the monetary union treaty itself was part and parcel of the end of geography thesis. This was Europe's response to the end of geography. There was going to be a single currency to match the single market, so that European companies would have a production platform and a currency stability from which to compete with the Japanese and Americans.

And they in their own context were also collaborators and competitors in this borderless world, so that the US has organised the North American Free Trade Agreement. And in Latin America states have gone through agonising adjustment programmes to meet the terms of IMF adjustment programmes—originating in the same thesis.

So the end of geography has led to colossal imbalances between the actual industrial structures of the major G7 states. It has led to a deflationary bias in policy and it has also led to political stasis, with a distrust of national politicians and political ideologies. It has become obvious to all, that, whatever they may say, politicians and national governments have not got ammunition to fight back in this world.

For example, British Aerospace has closed down 3,000 jobs in Hatfield—many of whom were Conservative voters, who are now coming to terms with the fact that the ideology of the party that they voted for is to permit low-cost production by British Aerospace in Taiwan. Both political parties have in a sense betrayed them and their community.

This kind of thing is happening on a huge scale. In France the EC reforms in agriculture, notwithstanding their necessity, are destabilising—a reason why French farmers voted so aggressively against the Maastricht treaty. Equally in Germany, with neither the CDU nor the SPD being able to come up with a plausible story of how Germany is going to deal with half a million refugees, there is a disaffection with politicians.

So the end of geography is so destabilising that we are collapsing back into a much more anarchic world, in which it is becoming apparent even to the authors of the thesis that it was not a particularly clever argument in the first place. But even at the height of the new ideology, the old impulses had never gone away. Privatisation was always described by the Institute of Economic Affairs or the Adam Smith Institute as privatisation—wherever it was. But privatisation meant many different things in different political and economic contexts.

In Britain privatisation meant selling state utilities back to their existing managements, turning them into joint stock companies owned by pension funds and insurance companies, and breaking the power of trade unions. That is not what privatisation meant in France. There the socialists and the right competed to make sure that the industrial financial holding company that became the beneficial owner of the former state enterprise was sympathetic to them.

In an Indian context privatisation is about ensuring that the Congress Party's grip on state patronage is reduced; while in South Africa the aim is to ensure that former strategically important public companies are held in white hands once power-sharing with the African National Congress begins. Privatisation in Poland is about ensuring that industries are not run by the old communist party or handed back to old nomenklatura. And one of the reasons why Poland is having such difficulty with privatisation is that excluding the nomenklatura is technically very problematic. In short, to argue that privatisation is just more proof that we live in a borderless free world sharing a common ideology has always been a thin argument; it serves political ends that differ in varying political circumstances.

Equally the story that the single market and monetary union treaty were part of a seamless web of European liberal integration was never very plausible. For surely the subtext of the events from 1987 to 1992 was that France was essentially trying to turn the Bundesbank into an institution whose direction France could share. The genesis of French proposals on the Monetary Union originate from the Basle/Nyborg agreements in which the Germans were compelled automatically to lend marks for up to three months under the short-term financing facilities of the European Monetary Corporation fund—a concession not made when the ERM was first founded.

But that was not good enough for the French. Kohl was armtwisted by Mitterrand to allow there to be a representative from the French Ministry of Finance sitting in on the Bundesbank council meetings. It became an immense political issue in Germany and he had to withdraw the proposal amid the uproar about the independence of the Bundesbank being compromised.

So back to the drawing board. Delors, Bérégovoy and Mitterrand then came up with the Monetary Union proposals, which were an attempt to entrench France as at least coequal partners in the running of monetary Europe. I met a Ministry of Finance official in Bonn last summer who recalled that the French supported their initiative by moving Hades missiles east of Paris—threatening not just Poland and Czechoslovakia, but large parts of Germany. The intent could hardly be clearer; and Kohl secured their withdrawal only when he accepted the idea of monetary union!

Similarly, Japanese Ministry of Finance officials have been very candid in private conversations, saying that if we want to understand Japanese monetary policy then we must understand the threats that came from the Pentagon about Japan continuing to enjoy American military protection.

Britain and the end of geography thesis

Yet this kind of thinking is very foreign in Britain; and when these explanations and linkages are offered—so that defence, trade, agriculture and finance all connect and that states actually play these cards—usually few take them seriously. There is a kind of Chatham House, Foreign

Office, Treasury view that more or less accepts that geography and history have ended, the world is borderless and these are the rules of the game.

But states remain ambitious to prosecute national goals and keep national institutions alive. And far from moving into a period of inter-national co-operation, in which the group of seven emerges as a kind of world government in exile with a permanent secretariat (floated at the Munich Summit in 1992), it is much more likely that the international trade and financial architecture will be pulled apart rather than pulled together. The world of competing nation states, with competition extend-ing to trade and financial relations with Japanese/US rivalry the epicentre, could get very serious.

Equally in Europe the forces between balkanisation around a united Germany and the hardening of the Franco-German alliance into an inner core are finely balanced. The key is the future of the ERM. If the French are forced to float, then the knock-on effects in terms of political union, monetary integration, agriculture and trade policy may be uncontainable. For the moment it looks as though the Bundesbank will cut interest rates rapidly enough to save the ERM—but the issue is not yet certain.

For British policy makers and British politicians, the issue is going to be whether we are going to change our institutions so that we can live inside the Exchange Rate Mechanism and all that means. Or are we going to believe that actually the end of geography thesis is right, that Britain should build its policy upon that basis; and that the EC will cease to integrate any further? The Conservative Party may even split over this and the strains on Labour are also intense.

But preparation for the ERM is an immense project which may be beyond us as a country. In political terms it requires the establishment of a rival political hegemony to contest the Conservative hegemony, and which will be able to introduce policies to reduce currency speculation, to sterilise the growth of liquidity in the banking system by introducing reserve requirement and to reform the labour market—maybe launching an incomes policy. And in the long run to make a new form of corporate governance work, together with reform of the entire financial system. The City of London is not going to go along with that.

Nor will it be supported by the 146 Tory MPs who represent Home Counties and outer-London constituencies, and the other 48 who represent the inner-London constituencies—what Galbraith calls the constituency of comfort. They want lower interest rates to keep the housing market moving. But equally importantly, their largely middle class electorate is in the process of decoupling itself from the social and economic institutions of the rest of the country—privatised schooling, health and pensions and looking for employment in multinationals and financial institutions whose business is predicated upon the world becoming more borderless. They want no part in a policy of national mobilisation to allow successful membership of the European core.

But will this fragmenting EC be happy to accept waves of exports of

Japanese cars and American computer companies from Britain? Will it accept Britain developing along free market, borderless world lines while it tries to preserve a social market economy? The omens are already not good, and as protection rises Britain runs the risk of being outside the two finance and trade blocs either side of the Atlantic.

Thus Britain and its politics are themselves a product of the Cold War, for the British middle class and Conservative Party could only develop their current economic and social options because of a world order that is now dead. On the other hand, Labour policies equally suppose a degree of British economic autonomy that no longer exists; and Labour shows few signs of recognising that to be successful it has to construct a political coalition that will contain the beneficiaries of economic mobilisation— from engineering companies to the regions outside the South-East. Instead it remains wedded to the politics of the manifesto, believing that if it can win a majority in the House of Commons it will govern a state that has the independence and power to act autonomously.

For the British the future of international co-operation is urgent, because in its absence Britain is one of the major losers. That must mean not merely willingness to participate in to European project, whatever it may be; but to redesign the country's economic and social institutions to conform to European norms. Things may have to get very much worse before the penny drops; and in the meantime the prospect is for an era of national competition in which nobody prospers, but where the strong can comfort themselves that they suffer least. Britain, the weakest, will suffer the most; but is the political class capable of absorbing the message? That very incapacity is part of the crisis.

INDEX

Adenauer, Konrad, 54, 55, 56
Albert, Michel, 1, 26, 46, 66, 99, 101–2, 105, 109
Anderson, Elizabeth, 14, 15
Anderson, Perry, 28
Andreotti, Guilio, 132
Arendt, Hannah, 62
Arts Council, 20
Associated Newspapers, 118
Association of Scientific, Technical and Managerial Staff (ASTMS), 117
AT&T, 34, 36, 42, 44
Australia, 37
Austria, 27, 54, 55, 56, 59, 60, 128

Baden-Württemberg, 133
Baldwin, Stanley, 129
Bangemann, Martin, 130
Bank of England, 141
Belgium, 54, 55, 56, 57, 59, 60, 127, 128, 133, 135
Bell Operating Companies, 44
Bellah, R. N., 62
Bérégovoy, Pierre, 143
Bevan, Aneurin, 25n
Block, Fred, 23
BOAC, 36
Boone Pickens, T., 72, 73
Bradford Metropolitan Council, 106
Bridgman Committee, 46
British Aerospace, 142
British Airways, 117
British Broadcasting Corporation, 33, 35, 94
British Gas, 117
British Leyland, 36, 71, 114
British Telecom, 39, 44, 116, 119, 123–4
Brittan, Sir Leon, 129, 130
BTR, 105
Bundesbank, 82, 84, 92, 132, 133, 139, 143
Burma, 138

Cable and Wireless, 39, 44, 117
Calabria, 133

Campbell, A., 104, 105
Catalonia, 133, 134
CDA (Netherlands), 61
Central Electricity Board, 36
Chandler, Alfred, 34
Chile, 32
CDU (Germany), 54, 142
City of London, 94, 144
Civic Forum (Russia), 127
Clarke, W., 38
Clinton, Bill, 2
Cockfield, Lord, 127
Committee of Regions, 133
Confederation of British Industry (CBI), 82, 126
Confédération Française Democratique du Travail (CFDT), 61
Congress Party (India), 42, 142
Conservative Party (UK), 97, 135, 144, 145
Coote, Anna, 30
Council of Ministers, 129, 130
Crick, Bernard, 62
Cronache Sociali, 58
Czechoslovakia, 46, 127, 143

Dalton, Hugh, 33
de Benedetti, Carlo, 133
De Gasperi, Alcide, 54, 55
Delors, Jacques, 61, 124, 127, 130, 143
Democrazia Cristiana (Italy), 54
Denmark, 85, 128, 136
Docklands Light Railway (London), 119
Donzelot, Jacques, 46

Ecole des Ponts et Chaussées, 39
Economic and Monetary Union (EMU), 133, 141, 143
Electrical, Electronic, Telecommunications and Plumbing Union (EETPU), 119
Engineering and Managers Association (EMA), 118

147

INDEX

Esping-Anderson, Gosta, 27
Esprit, 58
Etzioni, Amitai, 24, 26
European Central Bank, 133
European Community, 28, 56, 127–37, 139–40, 144–5
European Council, 130
European Free Trade Association (EFTA), 127
European Monetary System, 128, 132
European Parliament, 135, 136
European Trade Union Congress (ETUC), 130
Exchange Rate Mechanism (ERM), 97, 141, 143, 144

Fabian Society, 21
Ferranti, 105
Feruzzi, 135
Fiat, 135
Finland, 32
Fischer, W., 84
Flanders, 61, 85
Ford, 106
Forestry Commission, 35
Foucault, Michel, 42
Fox, A., 113
France, 31, 32, 33, 34, 39–40, 54, 55, 56, 57, 58, 59, 93, 101, 102, 127, 128, 133, 135, 138, 140, 142, 143, 144
Friedman, Milton, 7
Fukuyama, Francis, 21

Gaebler, Ted, 30, 46
Galicia, 133
GEC, 105
General Electric, 105
General Motors, 115
Germany, 27, 33, 34, 36, 46, 54, 55, 56, 57, 60, 78, 80–94, 97–8, 101, 102, 127, 134, 135, 139, 142, 143, 144
Gladstone, William E., 34
Goold, M., 104, 105
Granada TV, 20
Gray, John, 23
Greece, 128, 129, 133, 135, 136

Hall, Lord, 124
Hanson Trust, 105

Hayek, Friedrich, 7, 23
Hegel, G. W. F., 12, 84
Hewlett Packard, 105
Heyworth Committee, 35
Hirsch, F., 83, 98
Hirschman, Albert, 46, 62
Hirst, P. Q., 62
Honda, 114
Hungary, 127

IBM, 105, 117
ICI, 20
IG Chemie, 91
IG Metail, 91
India, 42, 138, 142
Institute of Economic Affairs, 22, 142
Ireland, 128, 129
Italy, 32, 54, 55, 56, 57, 58, 59, 60, 85, 127, 129, 133, 134, 135, 137, 140

Jaguar, 106
Japan, 1, 34, 42, 46, 68, 69, 70, 71, 72, 73, 74–5, 77, 79, 98, 140, 141, 143
John Paul II, Pope, 61

Kanter, R. M., 105
Keynes, John Maynard, 96
Kohl, Helmut, 139, 143
Koito, 73
Kuttner, Robert, 22

Labour Party (UK), 2, 82, 144, 145
Labour Research Department, 121
Latin America, 142
Liberal Democratic Party (UK), 2
Lijphart, A., 57
Lipsey, David, 21
Lombardy, 133
London Passenger Transport Board, 36
London Transport, 119
Lucas, 106
Luxembourg, 129

Maastricht Treaty, 129, 130, 133, 135, 142
McCarthy, Lord, 121
MacGowan Committee, 35
MacGregor, Sir Ian, 112
MacIntyre, Alasdair, 17
Macmillan, Harold, 32

Manchester Ship Canal, 32
Maritain, Jacques, 58, 63
Marquand, David, 24, 62
Marshall, Alfred, 37
Marx, Karl, 8, 11, 12
Matsushita, 105
Matzner, E., 81
Mayo, Elton, 122
Mercury Communications, 117
Metropolitan Water Board, 32
Mill, John Stuart, 53
Miller, David, 6
MITEL, 119
Mitterrand, François, 143
Monnet, Jean, 56
Monopolies and Mergers Commission, 73
Moran, Michael, 24
Moro, Aldo, 59
MRP (France), 60
Mumford, Lewis, 62
Myrdal, Gunnar, 62

National Bureau of Economic Research, 78
National Council for Vocational Qualifications, 107
National Economic Development Council (NEDC), 81, 127
National Graphical Association (NGA), 117
National Security Council, 140
National Trust, 94
National Union of Journalists (NUJ), 118
Nehru, Jawaharlal, 31
Netherlands, 54, 55, 56, 57, 58, 60, 61, 127, 128, 135
New Japan Steel, 71
News International Group, 117
Nkrumah, Kwame, 31
North American Free Trade Agreement, 142
Norway, 27
NTT, 42
Nussbaum, M., 49, 62

OECD, 78
Olivetti, 135
Osborne, David, 30, 46

Padoa-Schioppa, Tommaso, 127
Pakistan, 138
Perroux, F., 51
Pesch, H., 51, 58
Peters, T., 105
Peugeot Talbot, 106
Pfeffer, Naomi, 30
Pigou, A. C., 37
Pirelli, 135
Plant, Raymond, 24
Plessey, 106
Poland, 127, 143
Polanyi, Karl, 13, 30, 46
Portugal, 128, 129
Post Office, 32, 34, 36, 41, 46, 116
Pujol, Jordi, 134
Purcell, J., 104

Rawls, John, 62
Reich, Robert, 2
Reid Committee, 35
Rhone-Alpes, 133
Rolls Royce, 36, 106
Rome, Treaty of, 129, 130
Rosenvallon, P., 62
Rover Car Manufacturing Group, 114
Russia, 46, 127
Ryan, J. P., 51

Sagoff, Mark, 15, 16
Scandinavia, 1, 60, 93
Scharpf, Fritz, 23
Schumacher, Kurt, 54
Schuman, Robert, 56
Scotland, 133
Securities Exchange Commission, 98
Shaw, G. B., 36
Single European Act, 127, 134, 136
Single Market, 127, 128, 130, 131, 143
Smith, Adam, 37, 93
Society of Graphical and Allied Trades (SOGAT), 117
Society of Telecom Executives (STE), 118, 119
Sombart, Werner, 34
South Africa, 42, 142
Spain, 129, 133, 134, 135, 136
SPD (Germany), 54, 142
Storey, J., 105, 106

Streeck, W., 81
Sturzo, Luigi, 51, 58
Summers, Lawrence, 25
Sun Yat Sen, 31
Sweden, 27, 141
Switzerland, 82, 128

Taiwan, 31
Takeover Panel, 72
Tarmac, 105
Tawney, R. H., 62
Telecom Security Limited, 119
Thatcher, Margaret, 126, 127, 132
Therborn, Goran, 27, 30
Titmuss, Richard, 7
Todd, Ron, 120
Toyota, 70
Trades Union Congress, 112, 113, 121, 122, 135
Training and Enterprise Councils, 107, 108–9
Transport and General Workers Union (TGWU), 120, 121
Treasury (UK), 96, 133

UNICE, 130
United Automobile Workers Union (UAW), 115

United Kingdom, 1, 2, 22, 23, 25, 28–30, 31, 32, 34, 35–6, 39, 42, 67, 68, 69, 70, 71, 72, 73, 74, 77, 82, 85, 93–6, 101, 102, 103–4, 106, 107, 109, 110, 111–14, 117–24, 126–7, 129, 133, 135, 141, 142, 143–5
United States of America, 1, 2, 27, 31, 32, 34, 36, 40, 42, 61, 67, 68, 69, 70, 71, 72, 73, 74, 77, 78, 90, 93, 101, 102, 107, 109, 110, 111, 119, 120, 140, 141
University Grants Committee, 94

Vallance, Iain, 124
Vatican, 53
Vauxhall, 114, 115

Waigel, Theo, 139
Walzer, Michael, 6, 8–11, 13, 14, 15, 62
Waterman, R. H., 105
Western Union, 34
Whitbread, 106
Whyte, J. H., 58
Williams, Raymond, 33
Witt, U., 100